THE PSYCHOLOGIST
AT WORK

THE PSYCHOLOGIST AT WORK

AN INTRODUCTION TO EXPERIMENTAL PSYCHOLOGY

By

MARY R. HARROWER, Ph.D.

Select Bibliographies Reprint Series

BOOKS FOR LIBRARIES PRESS

FREEPORT, NEW YORK

First Published 1937
Reprinted 1969

STANDARD BOOK NUMBER:
8369-5128-X

LIBRARY OF CONGRESS CATALOG CARD NUMBER:
71-102243

PRINTED IN THE UNITED STATES OF AMERICA

Dedicated

to

K. K., A. B. *and* **I. M. H.**

WHO WERE ALL CONVINCED THIS BOOK

COULD BE WRITTEN

CONTENTS

ACKNOWLEDGMENT

IN the preparation of this book I am indebted to Miss Alison Mitchell for her drawings, to Miss Betty Boyd for her textual corrections and to Miss Alice Brown for her constant help and encouragement. Above all, I wish to express my gratitude to Professor K. Koffka, my teacher and colleague, for his invaluable constructive criticism and for the never-failing interest he has shown in this attempt to make experimental psychology accessible to the layman.

PREFACE

IF one believes that a general knowledge of modern academic psychology is part of an educated person's equipment no less than a general knowledge of modern physics and astronomy, one must welcome this attempt to introduce the psychologist's mode of thinking and experimenting to the general public. But even those who have nothing but a shrug of the shoulder for this youngest of sciences may change their minds when they read the author's presentation. Having spent in psychological work more years than I care to count, I find it very hard to judge the feelings of someone who meets psychology as it were for the first time; nevertheless, I believe that this book is both persuasive and convincing. Persuasive not in the sense that the author wants to enlist the reader's sympathy for any one of the many " isms " that divide psychologists into warring factions, but by the directness of its language which, as the sensitive reader will not fail to notice, is the manifestation of an underlying enthusiasm. I believe that the reader who has read the first chapter will not want to stop before he has finished the book. It is convincing, in that it shows that the problems

Preface

treated in psychological laboratories—and the author selects her material from a very wide field—are not artificial questions that yield either obvious or totally uninteresting answers, but demand to be solved if man wants to understand the universe and his place within it. For it is the great merit of the book that, although it uses simple language and does not pre-suppose any familiarity with its subject, it introduces the fundamental theoretical issues from the start, and that these main problems are never lost sight of in the detailed presentation of material.

The book is non-partisan and thoroughly fair, but it is not eclectic—the author is not afraid of telling her readers which solution she accepts as the most prob-able, the most fruitful. Naturally it is a particular pleasure to me that her general framework is that of Gestalt Theory.

K. KOFFKA.

PARIS,
25th July, 1937.

TO THE READER

I MUST first ask you a question: are you one of the general public for whom this book is written, or are you an experimental psychologist in your own right, ready to confront me with your superior knowledge on every page?

If you belong to the first-mentioned group I will only say that the chapters which follow, for better or for worse, are written for you. My hope is that you will gain from reading them some indication of the field in which the psychologist works, some of the questions he asks, some of the methods he uses, and the kinds of answers he is satisfied or dissatisfied with.

If, however, you belong to the second group, if you are as well equipped to write this book as I, then my foreword must take on a more serious tone. You may feel that, as an expounder of psychological problems, I have done things which I ought not to have done, and left undone things I ought to have done. The examples which you would have included at all costs you may not find, while my selection may seem a biased one to you. There may be places where you consider I have over-simplified, while there may be

To the Reader

other passages which it will seem to you that no layman can follow.

But if, as a result of reading these chapters, you are sufficiently stirred to write an account of the subject yourself, that will be excellent; for then the layman will have additional chances of learning about experimental psychology!

NEW BRUNSWICK, N.J.
June, 1937.

THE PSYCHOLOGIST AT WORK

CHAPTER I

THE PROVINCE OF PSYCHOLOGY

PROBABLY no one undertakes to write a non-technical account of any subject without finding that it is one fraught with particular difficulties; psychology is no exception. The difficulties, however, involved in psychology are, I believe, peculiar to it, and their enumeration may well serve as a starting-point.

In the first place, psychology suffers from the ease to which it lends itself to popular usage and exposition. Just because human beings are known to be in some way its subject matter, anyone and everyone feels that he has the right to use the term to describe his observations of himself and of his neighbours. The very fact that the word is used so indiscriminately in and of itself weakens its academic or scientific status.

And it is not only loose popular usage which has rightly made the average reader suspicious of the

term; popular magazines, newspaper articles and
even advertisements refer to its so-called problems
and solutions with such an assurance that the general
public is forced to accept as fact, even if with dis-
pleasure, what they feel at best to be a pseudo-science.

Any attempt at a non-technical discussion of psychological problems must first clear the ground of many
popular notions as they exist to-day, and must present
in their place problems sufficiently convincing, and
show methods sufficiently stringent to dispel the just
criticism of its pseudo-scientific nature.

Let us rule out of court, once and for all, some of
the things which psychology is *not*. We may group
the various false claims under several headings.
First, psychology, as studied by the serious student,
lays no claim to being a simplified rule of thumb,
ensuring more satisfactory lives to those who study
it. It does not claim to give clear-cut solutions to
the major problems of individual lives; it is not, as
I have seen claimed in print, ' a lifeboat on a mentally
troubled ocean ', nor can ' constructive psychology
bring a new day to America '. It is true, as we shall
see later, that our attitude towards life, or our everyday philosophy, to use a somewhat hackneyed term,
can be deepened and broadened by a fuller understanding of certain psychological laws, but that is a
different matter. No subject that we devote our lives
to, no branch of knowledge that we give time and
consideration to, can fail to influence our thought in
other fields. In this way undoubtedly our knowledge

of psychology can play into our more general approach to life ; but no study of psychology will equip us with a series of ready-made solutions to the questions which have troubled men throughout the ages, or guarantee a safe and sure course of action relevant to the needs and stresses of the moment. Psychology, in short, is no magic open sesame to knowledge which will render thought unnecessary thereafter.

Secondly, psychology as a branch of knowledge has no concern with bettering the worldly or economic status of the individual. I am thinking of such claims as those which guarantee eloquence, personality, magnetism, charm, wealth, confidence, remarkable memory and sundry other talents, to those who profit by the so-called findings of psychology. Neither, for that matter is academic psychology concerned with correcting individual bad habits, although undoubtedly methods may be developed incorporating its general findings, and applied in fields other than the psychologist's.

Thirdly, psychology is not a form of thought reading : a psychologist is not equipped to read his neighbour's mind, nor does he expect, on the basis of his training, to ' sum up ' a character at a glance.

Then, the subject-matter of psychology is not that of psychic research : psychology has virtually no connection with spiritualism, except in so far as spiritualism is an occupation in which human beings engage, and as such, that is, as an occupation, may be studied by the psychologist.

Lastly, psychology is distinct from psychiatry and psycho-analysis. This distinction, of course, does not belong to the foregoing illustrations of the misuse of the word psychology, but it is nevertheless puzzling to many people. The psychiatrist is a doctor, primarily concerned with abnormal mental states, insanity in its various forms and the maladjusted individual. The psycho-analyst, also concerned with maladjusted people, has gained his particular title because he believes in the therapeutic value of a certain method of treating such cases; namely, by using psychological analysis he attempts to bring to the surface hidden psychological difficulties.

Actually the layman's vocabulary bears evidence of the imprint of psycho-analysis to a greater extent than it bears the traces of psychology proper. Complexes, for example, have firmly entrenched themselves, and we have pigeonholed our friends with disastrous ease with the aid of 'inferiority' and 'superiority'. The libido, the censor, various sex symbols and an aroused interest in dreams, all these current literature and the layman have appropriated.

To come back, however, to the above-mentioned misconceptions; the ambiguity of the word in the popular usage is the psychologist's first difficulty; very often it will mean that he must start by creating respect for, or creating a belief in, the integrity of his subject before he can discuss it in proper terms. One has only to compare the layman's approach to the physical sciences, which he reveres and confesses his ignorance of, in order to see the difference in psychology's place in the opinion of the average reader.

But there is also another difficulty inherent in such a presentation of psychology. Let us again compare it with the physical sciences. Because of the just respect to which they are entitled, because their province is recognized as one requiring years of specializing and severe training, the layman approaches them with the knowledge that his ordinary everyday notions will have to give place to a new system of thought ; he realizes that the problems will be far removed from his everyday experiences, and he accepts this as right and proper. Science, he knows, is a realm in which one forfeits the obvious experiences of the world one lives in, experiences which seem self-evident and essential, in order to reach a more valuable and lasting understanding of the universe. It seems only right and proper to the layman that the physicist, for example, should talk to him about atoms, protons and electrons, convenient hypotheses for which there are no possible equivalent experiences. And it seems in keeping with the subject that its experiments be performed in the rarefied atmosphere of the laboratory.

But let the psychologist attempt the same thing ! A storm of protest reaches him at once. The idea of the ' human guinea pig ' is never taken seriously ; how, it is asked, can there be a controlled experiment with human beings when there will always be an indefinite number of uncontrollable and unknowable factors ? Abstractions and working hypotheses are not acceptable either, for they appear to make an unreal artefact out of something each reader knows only too well—himself.

Psychologists themselves are not entirely free from blame concerning this difficulty : the attempts to rid psychology of everything pertaining to common every-day experiences have in many cases been overdone. Psychologists have been so eager to get away from themselves in the capacity of ordinary individuals, and so eager to make a science of psychology at once, that they have tended to impoverish their own sub-ject-matter. Let us be more explicit about this behaviour which the layman feels must be artificial because it is conducted in a laboratory. If the truth were known, almost every student of psychology, every psychologist in embryo, feels disappointed when he realizes how few of his spontaneous questions psychology can answer. Even the knowledge that he is developing an accurate technique hardly compensates for the barrenness, the unimportance, the unrelated-ness of some of his first experiments. He may match different greys on a colour-wheel, a fast-revolving disc, may make a map of the pain, pressure, heat and cold ' spots ' on his arm ; he may try and classify smells, he may discover his partner's ' retinal blind spot ' ; or he may learn list upon list of nonsense syllables and repeat them at set intervals ! All too often the student's very natural desire to see *why* all this is of importance is allowed to drop into the background,

until finally it is replaced by the belief that in order
to be on a safe scientific basis he must confine his
interest to problems which are amenable to treatment
by a rather restricted technique.

It is not the aim of this book to justify every experiment committed in the name of science, or to pretend
that psychologists have never been blind to problems
of interest in their anxiety to give to their subject a
proper scientific status : it is rather to show *what* a
psychological problem is, to analyse for the reader his
ordinary everyday experiences, to re-examine what at
first sight appears to be the very warp and woof of
existence and beyond investigation, and to show that
here are problems, psychological problems, amenable
to isolation and control. It is our aim to examine
and evaluate some of the ' laboratory artefacts ', to
bring them, rather than the psychology of the popular
magazine, into the range of the general reader's thought,
and so to fit them into a more general framework,
that they will be seen as bricks, necessary in the
erection of that structure to which all branches of
knowledge contribute—the understanding of man and
the universe.

When we speak of fitting psychological facts into
a more general framework, the unique position of
psychology becomes apparent in another way. While
physics is concerned with inanimate matter, and
physiology with living tissue (which at the same
time incorporates many aspects of inanimate matter),
psychology embodies both physical and physiological

or biological principles, and at the same time contains something specific and unique—namely, mind. Since we shall frequently need to contrast psychological with both physical and physiological happenings, let us stop for one moment and be quite clear as to the distinction involved.

Take a very simple example : I pinch my finger in a door. When I describe what the door does, in terms of its weight, and the momentum with which it swings and so on, I am in the realm of physics. When I speak of the change in my skin, tissues, nerves and brain on account of the mechanically caused injury, I am within the province of physiology, but when I speak of what I *felt* as a direct result of these changes in skin, nerves, brain, etc., I am speaking of a psychological event. Moreover, it is well to remember that what I felt was pain-in-my-finger and I did not experience changes taking place in my skin, nerves and brain. This is a distinction which we shall need to use at various times in these chapters.

To return to our argument in the preceding paragraph, and to paraphrase a well-known modern psychologist : that with which psychology is concerned is the juncture, the meeting-place where inanimate matter, living tissue and mind are all concerned.

Now this statement immediately raises the question of just how these fields are related, of just how far we may expect new principles to be operative in each realm, of whether, in the last analysis, the fundamental laws are not the same in all. And depending

on our answer to this question we must be prepared
either to divorce psychological findings from the other
sciences, substantiating the claim for their treatment
within an altogether different framework, *or* to admit
them to be interlocked with the findings of science
on matter, organic and inorganic, living and dead,
and in consequence of this to make our very framework itself part of a much larger system of knowledge.

The first alternative means that irrevocable dividing-
lines exist in the world, such that no one type of
explanation can ever account for mind, the animate
and the inanimate. The second means that we are
concerned with the ultimate unification of all aspects
of the world as we know it, and assume that apparent
inconsistencies in such a scheme are due to gaps in
our own knowledge. Now since the character of our
framework for psychological findings, and the very
experiments which we consider important, will to a
large extent be dependent on our answer to this more
general question, it is well to make these alternatives
more explicit.

Our immediate feeling, it would seem to me, with
regard to these dividing-lines, is to make the gap
between inanimate things and living things the most
important, to feel that the factor of ' life ' in a very
real sense allows animals and human beings to be
grouped together in contradistinction to the world of
physical nature. But how about plants and the lower
forms of animal life ; and again, is the line between
our minds and our bodies to be drawn so emphatically ?

It is clear that the exact position of these demarcations presents difficulties.

In regard to the second alternative, namely, that there are in reality no such dividing-lines, we can see immediately that two types of unification are possible —either we explain mind in terms of the laws, as we know them, that govern inanimate nature, or we work in the other direction and read the characteristics of mind into physical nature. This last we find very often in the world of primitive man and of children ; thunder and lightning, wind and fire and so forth become personified, and motives are detected in their operations.

This type of explanation in its primitive form we can dismiss altogether ; but we must now consider seriously the most clear-cut cases of our two alternatives, namely, the mechanistic or materialistic theory, and the theory which we will call in contradistinction to it, vitalistic, ' vitalistic ' in that it maintains that there will always be a ' vital factor ' necessary for our understanding of ' life ', *per se*, over and above all explanations which may be contributed to our understanding of the human and animal body by the other sciences.

How does the materialist explain his position ? He is convinced that all behaviour, human and animal, is explicable solely in mechanical terms, that science will eventually give us such a clear understanding of this human machine that we shall be able to predict and control human action in the same way as we can guarantee the specific performance or function of any man-made apparatus. He will point to the structure of the human nervous system and will illustrate and emphasize its machine-like qualities, for instance, its numerous conducting pathways which are in essence so similar to a man-made telephone system. He will refuse to allow our wills or our thoughts to be in any way determining factors in our behaviour, claiming that the way the ' machine ' is made will determine the action of the given individual, and that these ' experiences ' are quite illusory in character. The A B C of his beliefs can be seen in the simple units of nerve action, a sort of penny in the slot idea, or turn on the switch and the lamp is lit. He argues that in each case there is a specially prepared pathway down which the ' penny ', in this case the nervous current, can travel and achieve its prescribed and predictable end. Nothing fundamentally different therefore is required to explain human behaviour ; in fact, man is simply a complicated machine.

Now the vitalist's platform is that, notwithstanding the attractive simplicity of such a scheme, notwithstanding the fact that the nervous system is a network of pathways down which excitations, or ' pennies ', of nervous energy do travel, yet man will always remain essentially unmachine-like, or perhaps super-machine-like because there will always be a ' something ', a vital force or ' spirit ' that will *direct* the action of the machine, that will use the machine so to speak, but will not be part of it. The vitalist claims that there is a purposefulness about human and animal behaviour that a machine can never achieve, that its overcoming of difficulties defies all mechanical explanation. And for every experiment which the mechanist can give to show that no new principle is needed to explain behaviour, the vitalist can produce one which reduces the machine-like aspect of man to a minimum.

With the outline of these two different general frameworks, the two apparently fundamentally different beliefs about the ultimate character of the results of psychological research, we have raised another question : namely, the relation of facts to theories. For we may well ask if, holding the mechanistic view, one is not *in consequence* led to discover facts in tune with it, led to plan experiments which will tend to corroborate it ; or, granted that one holds to the vitalistic approach, will one not seek out just such experiments as will disprove the claims of the mechanist ? In other words, the reader may well ask if every psychologist is not unwittingly predisposed towards one or the other of these approaches : he may wonder how one can guarantee that facts are not selected to fit theories, or theories developed utilizing only certain facts, in order to satisfy a deep-seated and inexplicable belief concerning the nature of things.

Let us admit that this is a possibility and be on our guard, let us admit that in both mechanism and vitalism an inevitable selection of, or rather interest in, certain types of questions exists, such that men are drawn to formulate the necessary experimental problems in order to provide a test case for a theory which has, in its turn, grown out of, or been necessitated by, other experimental material. But must we say that it does not matter which framework we select for a discussion of experimental problems since both can be substantiated? Must we admit that our foundations and framework are unstable because there is no decisive answer in favour of either approach?

Consider the two alternatives again; where, if at all, are they unsatisfactory? Mechanism is unsatisfactory to the unbiased reader, I believe, because it is not only an outrage to common sense, but also because it makes all knowledge, even to the ' discovering ' of the mechanistic framework itself, quite useless and arbitrary! If the particular constitution of my nervous system is such that I *must* ' discover ' a mechanical theory to be satisfactory, what is the value of such a discovery?

The inadequate nature of vitalism is perhaps less obvious, because at first sight it seems to take care of the disconcerting gap left by mechanism, and admits of essentially human values in their own right. But its disadvantage lies in the fact that by definition it excludes from scientific treatment the very crux of the matter. In other words, it claims that this ' life essence ' can never be caught in the mechanist's explanatory net because it is a different *kind* of entity; but in doing this it virtually assumes that the psychologist's problems can never be available to

scientific treatment either, since the very ' stuff
which they are made of ' defies explanation in
these terms.

At this point we seem to have come to what looks
like an impasse ; for we have rejected both of our
alternatives, which seem to epitomize points of view
which are diametrically opposed ; and if we find
satisfaction in neither, what have we to suggest ?
Perhaps we may ask, are these points of view as
fundamentally different as they appear at first sight,
or is it not possible to see in both mechanism and
vitalism a common element, and in suggesting an
alternative to this common factor to find that we
have broken new and promising ground ?

. I believe it is possible, for mechanism and vitalism
both assume, both accept as a matter of course, the
essentially machine-like properties of the body. The
vitalist, while insisting that purposive behaviour cannot arise from such a body alone, none the less en-
visages the additional ' vital spirit ' as directing a
purely mechanized body. So, as a first formulation
of a third alternative, we might say : is not perhaps
the over-mechanical conception of the body in itself
to blame ? Might it not be possible after all to catch
psychological phenomena scientifically when we have
a different kind of ' explanatory net ' ? Might not
another kind of unified approach be possible, a unification along lines other than those we have described as
mechanistic ?

What do these general statements mean ?   What is

the 'mechanistic type of concept' and what would we substitute in its place?

If we think of any kind of man-made machine we can discover two very general aspects: power (in whatever form, electric, steam, pressure of the hand, etc.), and those restrictions or constraining parts which send the power in the right direction.

If there were no water-*pipes* for example, how would the water, under pressure, reach its destination, its required or orderly destination? If there were no pistons in an engine, how would the steam, under pressure, produce the required turning of the wheels? If the keys of my typewriter, or of the piano, were not held in place, how could the pressure of my fingers ensure their striking the paper or the strings? The result of all this is that our inevitable implicit conclusion about how a machine works is that unless you harness force, unless you restrict it, the orderly or required result will not be obtained: and this implicit conclusion about machines carries over into our ideas about physical forces in the world in general, in such a way that we look on the forces of nature as chaotic, disorderly, incapable of arriving at any kind of harmonious or controlled pattern unless they also are restricted and harnessed and directed to a certain end.

But we who are looking for another type of concept, what have we to say to all this which is undoubtedly true? The answer is: the machine-like type of orderly happenings, despite its prevalence in our everyday world, is by no means the only type of order in nature. To achieve certain calculated ends for man's particular and specific purposes, undoubtedly this sort of orderly functioning is essential, but it is by no means the inevitable characteristic of physical nature everywhere in the universe that it cannot achieve order except through the channels of machine-like constraints. In short, it frequently happens that the forces of nature can, and do, ' work them-selves out ' to produce order and arrangement, har-mony and pattern, independently of any rigid con-straints such as are looked on as order-producing in a typical machine.

A machine has what is called ' one degree of freedom ' and the uniformity and regularity of its action depend on just this fact. The action of the penny-in-the-slot machine, for example, is guaranteed because there is only one tree direction in which it can move. We usually contrast this type of action, the inevitable order of a system with one degree of freedom, with our own or animal action, assuming that when orderly action results with more than one degree of freedom, something other than physical nature must be in-volved, a something which may be said to select or choose that direction which will produce orderly behaviour or action.

What we are emphasizing now is that orderly results are in actual fact achieved in nature itself *even when* more than one degree of freedom is in-volved in the system.

Now it is necessary here to give concrete examples, but it is even more necessary to be sure that this discussion is seen, not as a digression, but as actually leading to those very concepts the existence of which may solve our problem with regard to our general approach to psychology.

We were evaluating mechanism and vitalism ; we found that mechanism failed to satisfy many of us because, for the sake of a simplified unification, it had reduced man to a machine ; but suppose we could show that in physical nature, ' freedom ' and essentially *un*machine-like action exist, and *yet* order-liness and harmony, should we feel so loath to find the barriers diminishing between ourselves and other aspects of our ' mysterious universe ' ? Similarly, if our new concepts did justice to, that is, did not need to explain away, or reduce to lower terms the essentially ' vital ' and the essentially ' human ' properties, we should not need to safeguard these by declaring them beyond explanation, as the vitalist is forced to.

Let us look at some concrete examples : the planetary system is perhaps the most striking. Here we have orderly functioning without any of the constraints, props or barriers which are essential in ' harnessing the forces ' of nature in a machine. No structure holds the stars in position, nor do they move along tracks which keep them in their courses. But their ' pre-established harmony ' and orderliness have been a by-word through the ages ; in fact,

this regularity was for a long time ' accounted for
by their crystal spheres the turning of which was
supposed to force the stars to move in their orbits'.
Men postulated a machine-like arrangement because
they could not conceive of an orderly system without
one.

Let us take another example, before we discuss what
the properties of the universe are which achieve this
non-mechanical order. If you put a drop of oil in
a glass of whisky it retains its shape and remains as
an entity. Why ? Certainly no physical barriers
exist between it and the whisky ; why then does it
not immediately disperse as, say, a drop of ink in
water ? Although these examples are drawn from
events of very different orders of magnitude, they
both can tell us a great deal about orderly performances other than mechanical ones. In these cases
we have no question of one degree of freedom : there
are *no* physical or mechanical restrictions in either
case ; consequently, theoretically, the number of
positions to which each star, or each particle of the
oil could move, is infinite. If the restrictions are
non-existent, then the regular orbits in the one case,
and the retaining of shape and entity in the other,
must be the result of *the actual property of the forces
involved* in each case ; and this, in fact, is the burden
of our non-mechanical song, the beginning of the
non-mechanical type of concept. Inherent in the
planetary system itself are forces which make for
orderly action. Inherent in the drop of oil are forces

which give it inner cohesion and retain its unbroken surface against the whisky. One might almost say that the particles of the oil ' wanted ' to stay together, because out of all the millions of possible positions for its individual particles, just that occurs which retains the drop's identity. Actually, of course, we would never suspect the oil of being guided by any ' spirit ' outside its own nature, and yet its behaviour is such as might suggest that, if we restrict orderliness of behaviour to some guiding outside agent.

Let us give one more example of a slightly different kind before we reiterate what all this has to do with psychology. It is obvious that the stars and the drop of oil behave in an orderly fashion, but there are also cases where we should find just the same type of non-mechanical order exhibited, if we only knew enough about the event to recognize it when we saw it. Take an everyday occurrence ; I spill some water on a hard polished floor. What happens ? The patch of water assumes a shape ; and, on the face of it, one certainly would consider this shape a purely chance affair. (If, in contradistinction, I had to say what I would consider an orderly or non-chaotic shape, it would probably be a square, a circle, a straight line, or some of our very familiar conceptions of orderliness. Moreover, if water always marshalled itself into one of these well-known shapes, say a square, whenever it was left to distribute itself, the idea of the essential irregularity of nature would not have so strong a hold.) But, to return, the fact

remains that, even though I am not familiar with
the particular shape assumed by the water on any
given occasion of my spilling it, that particular shape
is an orderly one ; that is, it is óne of the shapes,
which out of millions of other possible ones has been
decreed by the forces involved in this particular case.
The force with which you spill the water, the amount
of water, the hardness of the floor, the slight irregularity in the plane of the floor, etc., all these combine
so that the water takes up a shape, and only that
shape, which brings about an equal surface tension
all over it, or in ordinary terms, makes out of it a
system where the forces are evenly distributed throughout.   Now there are, undoubtedly, many different
orderly shapes which the water may assume, depending
on these different conditions.   But, in contradistinction
to a machine, we see that all restraining guarantees
of order are lacking, that is, there are no barriers
on the floor to hold the water in this particular shape,
or guide it into it.   And yet an orderly performance
has been achieved, ' selected ', we might almost be
tempted to say again, because properties in the water,
and the act of spilling, and the floor, are, in their own
way, as compelling as the restraints of a machine.

Now let us pull together our non-mechanical ideas
concerning the non-mechanical aspects of nature and
see where they will help us in psychology.   For the
reader may still ask, " But why is this so important,
even if things do ' move under their own steam '
more than we thought they did ?   Why, even if

nature does achieve results more interesting and complex than those of a machine, should that affect us ? ''

The answer to this question will, in one form or another, permeate this whole book, but at this stage, and relevant to this discussion of a general framework, we may say : why should the mechanist in an attempt to make psychology scientific, in an attempt to use only accredited scientific terms and procedure, limit those terms to one aspect only of physical nature ? Why, for example, should his descriptions of man's behaviour be more automatic than the accurate description of the performance of the spilt water ? If we must admit non-mechanical action and order achieved with more than one degree of freedom, in *inanimate* things, why deny such concepts when dealing with *man* ? In other words, the mechanist when he eliminates all except the machine-like explanation of man's behaviour in order to bring it into line with the physical sciences, is overlooking one of the very important parts of the physical sciences themselves and making his standards from only one small province of the working of inanimate things. In order to be in line with science we do not need to reduce man's actions to the automatic, penny-in-the-slot-machine type.

Now these same non-mechanical concepts help us also in our answer to vitalism, because, if we use them, we provide ourselves with what I called ' another type of explanatory net with which to catch our facts '. If we can show that orderly functioning is

just as much a part of the planets as is their mass
and structure, why should the essentially orderly
functioning or behaviour of man be split off from man
himself and considered beyond explanation? If we
do not need to reduce to lower terms those phases
of behaviour which common sense tells us plainly are
not automatic, why should we not include them in
our scientific investigations on man? For these
psychological phenomena, even if they cannot be
caught in a test-tube, or held under a microscope,
may in their turn throw light on that which can,
just as the behaviour of the drop of oil in the whisky
tells us something about the composition of the oil.

And so the general framework which we shall adopt
will be something like this : man's behaviour, man's
mind, man's experiences, all of which are the psychologist's province, do not need to be considered as
separated by an unbridgeable gulf from the more
tangible phenomena of the physical sciences, for we
may find in them indications of the same laws which
govern other aspects of both man and the universe.
Furthermore, just as a detailed and relatively isolated
problem in one branch of science can throw light, not
only on general problems in its own field, but may
also be illuminating in allied sciences, so we may
hope that detailed studies of behaviour and experience
made by the psychologist may likewise contribute to
the more general problems concerning man and his
environment.

The list of books and articles appended to each chapter indicate the sources from which the material and the quotations of the text have been taken ; and also include more general references bearing on the questions under discussion.

Page 4. See Flugel's article on Psycho-analysis in *Psychologies of 1930.* Ed. C. Murchinson, Worcester, Mass.

„ 8. Cf. K. Koffka, *Principles of Gestalt Psychology*, Chap. I. New York and London, 1935.

„ 11. For a presentation of Vitalism in psychology see H. Driesch, *The Crisis in Psychology.* Princeton, N. J., 1925.

„ 15 ff. Cf. W. Köhler, *Gestalt Psychology.* Chap. IV. New York and London, 1929.

„ 18. The quotation is from Köhler, *loc cit.*

CHAPTER II

HOW WE SEE OUR WORLD

WE have discussed what psychology is not, and have
tried to construct a general framework within which
the experimental facts can be seen ; with this in mind
we are now ready for that analysis of our everyday
experiences, for that re-examination of what seems to
be the very warp and woof of existence, with which
these chapters are chiefly concerned.

It is not difficult to describe these experiences, they
are such common property ; the difficulty lies in
translating them into ' problems '. My immediate
experience at this moment, for instance, is the room
in which I am writing, the paper and pen which I
am seeing and feeling, the chair in which I am sitting,
which I also see and feel, the room in front of me
with its cream-coloured walls and pictures on them,
its coloured carpet, its chairs and tables, the lamps,
one near me and one farther away. My experience
also contains sounds in the street outside, and the feel
of the wind from the open window.

Let us take one aspect of my immediate experience,
or of my consciousness, at a time : the things I see,

Unquestionably they constitute the most important part of my world at the present moment, or shall we say, to deprive me of them would impoverish my world most drastically. These *things*, these shapes, these sizes, these colours, these distances, these lights and shades : how is it possible that I experience them ?

" It is possible," you will be tempted to answer without delay, and in the hopes of preventing me from

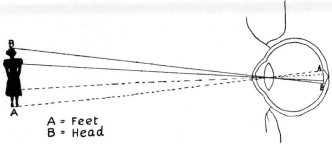

A = Feet
B = Head

FIG. 1.

making much ado about nothing, " because we have eyes." " All right," I will answer, " how do eyes make these experiences possible ? " " I know that too," you may reply, " and I can even draw you a diagram of it ; the eye has a lens like a camera, the rays of light are focused on the retina, that is, on the sensitive surface behind the lens, equivalent to the film or plate in the camera, and an exact image of the object is formed, and of course, in consequence I see it."

" Very good," I can reply, " but not so fast. You talk as if ' you ', or some part of you, saw another part of you, or looked at that little image on the retina. But that you cannot mean, because in the first place, that little image is upside down, you yourself have pointed out its similarity to the image on the plate of a camera ; secondly, it is but a fraction of the size of the object in the room, the object you experience the seeing of. Moreover, that little image on the retina is inside your head at the back of your eyes, but your experience is of something which is outside you, in the room. Finally, and just to show you how difficult this question is going to become, I shall show you that there might be a little image on your retina and yet you would not ' see ' the object, and I could even make you see something when there is no little image on your retina."

" But," you will say in desperation, " my seeing has *something* to do with the image on my retina, because, for all your talk, when I close my eyes and shut out the image, I don't ' see '."

Now I am in full agreement with you, and you have saved me the trouble of formulating one of the main problems in the psychology of vision when you say ' something ' to do with those light rays, striking and focused on the retina. For it is the task of the psychologist to examine all his experiences of sight very closely to see what connection exists between them and the physical happenings in the world outside him. Let us go back one step. What is the difference between my *experience* when I sit in my chair with my eyes closed, and when they are open? We may distinguish between stages one and two in terms of both actual happenings in the world and experiences. In the world of happenings when I have my eyes shut, the light rays which are reflected from all the surfaces of all the things in the room, fall on my eyelids (as they also strike all the rest of my body) and are simply reflected back again into the room. When my eyes are open, however, these same rays which struck my lids before, now pass through the lens of my eyes and, as you have mentioned, are drawn together and focused at a certain distance behind the lens because of the properties of the lens through which they pass. The difference in *happenings* in the room, then, between stage one and two is very small; a minute amount of the light changes its course in a very slight way, converging at one point instead of being diffused and scattered.

But the difference in my experience is enormous! It could mean all the difference between a knowledge of the world we live in and perpetual darkness. Even though the miracle of seeing our world has become commonplace, it is still possible for all of us to compare the complete, rich, varied and interesting experience of seeing, even our own rooms, with the blankness and crampedness of keeping our eyes shut, or not seeing. An insignificant change in physical happenings, then, parallels the immense change in our experience. "But," you will say, "there is still some change, I

must still believe that ' somehow ' the little image
brings me my experience of the world I live in.''

At this point we have to be very careful; in fact,
it could be said that if you understand the *problem*
involved here, you may consider yourself a psychologist from now onward ! It is all too easy to assume
that the things which we see must *themselves* be respon-
sible for our seeing them, because images of them
must be formed on our retinæ.   But actually our only
connection, our only contact with the outside world
as far as sight is concerned, is through the rays of
light which travel *from* the things, from that chair,
let us say, to our eyes. It so happens that each
minute point on the chair reflects light, and each of
these rays strikes my retina ; but the wall behind the
chair, and the floor under it and the table at the side,
every point on all of these is reflecting light also, and
as each individual light ray hits the retina it does so
independently of all the other light rays, and carries
with it no indication that it belonged to either chair,
table, wall or floor ; it simply hits its target and does
its inevitable duty as if fired off a point on the surface
of the chair on to the sensitive surface of the eye.
In other words, when we talk about an image on the
retina as if it were a coherent unit, we are muddling
up our world of experiences (for undoubtedly we
experience images, and things, as coherent units) with
the world of happenings.   But we have to remember
that the retina of the eye, as a physical substance, in
the physical world, is simply being subjected to

millions and millions of isolated pinpricks, to a battery
of light rays fired independently of each other from
all the reflecting surfaces of the room.

Consequently our first problem goes one stage further
back than seems at first sight needful. The question
is not, How does this minute, inverted image of the
chair on the retina become the chair of my experience ?
but, How does it happen in the very beginning that the
light rays from unified objects in the outside world
give rise to unified objects in my experience ? Because,
as each of these light rays travels through space, and
as each independently rings up its mark, so to speak,
on the retina, they are quite unrelated one to another.
The light ray which comes from the very edge of the
chair, its one neighbour which has been reflected from
the wall, and its other neighbour which also comes
from the chair, these units are all equally unrelated.
Only through ' magic ', or through something happening in the organism, can the change in character
of what we see, as opposed to what is there on the
retina, be accounted for.

And of course we do not need to resort to magic ;
for your organism, your eyes, nerves, and brain which
are going to participate in the seeing, which are going
to utilize this information from the outside world,
your organism ' does something ' very important with
these isolated messages which it gets ; namely, it is able
to group together certain bits of information, into the
' right ' groups we might say, unaided by any one
isolated part of that information in itself.

In other words, ' seeing ' is not merely the result of an image imposed by the outside world ; that we can see an ' image ' in the first place is an achievement of the organism, largely dependent on certain properties which, as an organism, as a living system, it possesses.

Before we go on to discuss the resulting psychological aspects of this achievement, before we can turn to the experimental work, we have to make explicit a hypothesis which is inherent in all we have been saying. Frankly, it is a hypothesis of the kind that we spoke of in Chapter I, of the kind that is treated with greater respect in the orthodox sciences, but which in psychology may appear as an irrelevant abstraction, unnecessary and even far-fetched. We advance it at this stage because it gives us an idea to play with, a ' something to work on '.

So far the burden of our song has been : our experiences are extraordinarily unlike the particular events in the physical world which are none the less the first link in the chain of their production. The question is, are we just to shrug our shoulders and say, this investigation has done nothing more than reinforce our original opinion that the experience of vision is little short of a miracle, and so unlike in *kind* anything that science can show to have ' caused ' it, that we might as well give up investigating ? Or can we gain any help by making some hypothesis about the intermediate link in the chain, namely, the physiological processes in the eye, nerves and brain, processes

which are set into operation directly by these light
rays which make their point of contact on the retina ?
Of course it is this second alternative that we shall
attempt. We have spoken several times now about
the intrinsic properties of certain kinds of systems in
nature in which orderly processes were established, in
which certain parts 'belonged together' and kept
themselves segregated from others. Now the hypothesis we need at this stage is that the organism is
just such a system, a system which is itself capable of
grouping and segregating the mosaic, pinprick type of
excitations that come in, capable of doing so, not by
magic or by chance, but because it possesses these
properties inherent in its very nature.

If we accept such a hypothesis it means that our
experiences are no longer 'totally different in kind'
from the events which immediately precede them ; for
these physiological events in question will *also* be
segregated, grouped, patterned wholes, and there is no
discrepancy in the idea of segregated processes giving
rise to the experience of segregated things.

With such a suggestion, then, we have lessened the
gap between the world of experience and the happenings in the nervous system, but there still remains the
gap, or difference in kind, between these orderly
segregated physiological processes and the unrelated
happenings in the ether with their pinprick contact
on the retina. But this need not be disquieting, for
the ether is in no sense a system with interrelated
parts as is the human organism, although as you know,

there are such interrelated systems in the physical world, as for example those mentioned in the last chapter.

Now this hypothesis, apart from the fact that it affords us an opportunity to lessen the gap which exists in our chain of explanation from light rays to ' seeing ', has another advantage. For if we assume this essential similarity between experience and the physiological processes in the nervous system, then what we know about these processes can help us to understand our experiences and vice versa. And this is in itself a valuable method because each set of facts, consciousness or experience on the one hand, and physiological processes on the other, can supply us with something that the other lacks. We mentioned this important difference in Chapter I, but perhaps we may re-state it briefly in this connection. I can never, for instance, know ' directly ' about the physiological processes in my eye, nerves and brain, that is, I can never know these happenings in myself *as processes*. What I do know directly is the experience (say of moving my arms, of being in the room, and so on) which results from them. If I wish to know about these processes, as such, I have to study them in some other organism, in animals or in living parts of animal tissue, and I have to watch, outside me, how these things happen. I am interested in how one event in one part of the tissue leads to another somewhere else, in tracing a sequence of cause and effect.

But when I come to consciousness the position is

reversed. I know it directly, from the ' inside ', so to
speak ; but it is when I want to explain it, when I
want to be able to say ' this led to that ', when I look
for cause and effect that the trouble begins. For into
what realm am I to go for such an explanation ?

Now on the assumption that there is an essential
similarity in the workings of the organism, as manifested in consciousness and as manifested in its physiological processes, we are justified in using a gain in
our knowledge in one realm as possibly significant
in the other, and at the same time have got some help
on the vexed question of what can be said to precede
or ' cause ' consciousness.

The full significance of this hypothesis cannot become evident until we have given actual examples :
the testing of it, therefore, will be one of the general
ideas which we shall hold in mind when we give illustrations of some of the psychologist's concrete experiments. However, we have come far enough, step by
step, I think, for you to be able to agree with me when
I ask my original question again, " How do I experience these things in my room ? " that the simple
obvious answer " Because of the image on the retina "
was nothing more than a short cut to the problem.
You will be able also to agree to a rather more detailed
definition of a psychological problem : it is not only
that the psychologist examines his experiences of sight
" to see what connection exists between them and the
physical happenings in the world outside him ", but,
rather more accurately we may say, he is interested

in determining the exact relationship between the properties of our visual experiences and the properties of the processes in the nervous system, and the relation of these same processes to the events in the physical world.

The first experiment therefore which we will discuss must be one to illustrate a number of things ; since we will describe it in detail it must be typical of the psychologist's methods when studying vision. Secondly, it must throw light on the characteristics of those physiological processes occurring in the organism which give rise to, or accompany, the visual experiences, for we must have good reasons for even suggesting the kind of hypothesis outlined above. Thirdly, such an experiment must show concretely, rather than by argument, the inadequacy of the ordinary conception that the little image on the retina of the eye is the answer to the question of why we see.

We have called it an ' experiment ', but perhaps in fairness to the psychologist we ought rather to say demonstration in this particular case, for a real experiment on this problem would have to ask more questions, and make more systematic variations, than we shall describe here.

However, let us suppose that you are now entering the psychological laboratory : since you are to take part in this ' experiment ' you are called a ' subject ', and all your remarks and comments will be written down in the experimenter's ' protocols ' on a page bearing your name.

You sit down in a chair at one end of a long bare room, and face an apparently plain white wall at the other. The experimenter then tells you that he is going to make the room dark and wants you to look in front of you and describe exactly what you see. The room is darkened completely, and you report: " I see a small moving bar of light ; it is about two inches long, about half an inch wide, and it is jumping backwards and forwards across a space of about five inches. It appears at the right-hand side, and jumps to the left, returns to the right and so forth in steady alternation. With that, in this particular demonstration, the experimenter tells you that this is all he needs you for : thank you. You are perhaps disappointed that so little of spectacular interest has occurred ; and to the experimenter's statement that if you only understood the problem you would see how important it all was, you reply with spirit that you are prepared to understand what he can tell you.

As a first step in the explanation, then, he will ask you to go up and see what in actual fact you have been looking at. At the far end of the room you find that there is a white cardboard screen attached to the wall which covers an opening into another room. In this screen, seven inches apart, are two small slits two inches in length and half an inch wide. Behind the screen in the other room are two strong lamps, on separate electric circuits. Between these lamps, attached and at right angles to the white screen, is a high wooden partition, which you can see prevents the light from the left lamp from shining through the slit on the right side and vice versa.

But, you ask, where is the screen that made possible the seeing of the one bar of light which moved all the way across the five-inch space? The answer is that there is no such screen. But, you protest, you saw the light move across the intervening space as clearly

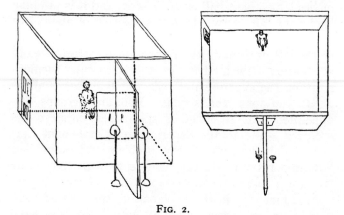

FIG. 2.

as you now see the two independent slits! That remark pleases the experimenter, for this means that you have seen a moving bar of light when no image of that moving bar existed on your retinæ.

Now the reason why this particular occurrence is of interest psychologically is that you have seen something which, on the face of it, you could not have seen, and have not seen what you should have seen. By

this I mean that the only images which could have
been on your retinæ were those corresponding to the
two bright little slits in the screen. If a camera plate
had registered what it ' saw ' under the circumstances,
it would have exhibited the two small bars of light ;
but you saw *movement*, and yet no moving light
existed, and no moving image crossed your retinæ !
What happened then ? Physically, in the experimental procedure, after the room was made dark, the
experimenter set his apparatus working so that each
of the two lamps behind the screen went on and off
independently for a fraction of a second, with a corresponding fractional pause of darkness between them.
This means that the two little bright areas on each of
your retinæ were stimulated, one after the other in
quick succession, over a period of time ; and since, in
a living system, what happens in one part will affect
what happens in another, the net result of this double
stimulation was something more than if each had been
stimulated alone. In what way might they affect
each other ? We must make another hypothesis : the
process starting as the result of the second stimulated
area might draw towards itself the process started at
the first, and might fuse with it. Then the result in
the system would be one shifting process, with the concomitant psychological characteristic of ' movement
between two areas '. With such a hypothesis we have
at least some explanation for what was incomprehen-
sible before ; for our experience of movement bears no
remote resemblance to two isolated streaks of light

(which is all that we receive in the way of information from the physical world) but may more readily be thought of as being the direct counterpart of the ' pull ' of one process on another and of their fusion.

Let us look at this experiment once more to see if it has fulfilled the conditions which we demanded from it. Why was it typical? Chiefly because, as it stands, without knowing what we are investigating there is nothing exciting about it, but with the knowledge of the point in question it can become dramatically meaningful. That this is true of almost all scientific experiments is sometimes forgotten by the layman who is inclined to demand the spectacular from psychology. It is typical also in its general pattern; the fact that it is so ' simple ', only two little bars of light in a dark room, is carefully planned : we want to be able to control all the factors involved, or as many of them as we can. If we know all that we can about the happenings in the physical world, then we can more accurately determine the peculiar characteristics of the world of our experience.

In the physical world in this experiment we know that in otherwise ' empty ' darkness there are two areas of physical energy, light rays of a controlled intensity, quality and duration of time. In this case the difference between the happenings in the physical and psychological world was startling, but unless you knew about the physical ' set-up ', as it is called, you would not have known that there was anything interesting in what you saw. This almost artificial simplicity is sometimes apt to disappoint even students of psychology unless the more general issues are kept in mind. This particular experiment, however, has an obvious connection with larger issues as our second and third questions show.

Our hypothesis about the nervous system and nervous processes leads us straight back to the question " Is man a machine ? " For here, in the result of this experiment, are some of the foundation stones for the building of our non-mechanical concepts. What is happening in the organism, even at this ' low level ' of elementary behaviour, of just seeing, is not a penny-in-the-slot-machine type of occurrence : rather there is evidence of processes which possess more than one degree of freedom.

The answer to our third question is perhaps the clearest of all : there is not the slightest doubt that we see something when there is no image on the retina to correspond to that particular thing. Two stationary bars of light are not the same as one moving one.

If you are sceptical about this isolated ' experiment ', or if you doubt whether you would have seen the movement that the hypothetical observer did, just think of an experience with which you yourself are familiar, the movies ! Here, as in the experiment, separate stationary pictures are projected on your retina, but you experience smooth, convincing movement. And this movement, which is ' manufactured ' by your organism and has no physical counterpart, and no direct retinal stimulation, is just as real a part of our psychological experience as are the lights and shades, which are given directly.

Or, if you wish to try something of a more experimental nature in order to convince yourself, arrange some long object, a tall stick for instance, and two lamps so that two shadows of the stick are cast on the wall several inches apart. Now switch one lamp off and on : one shadow will be seen as jumping away from the other as the lamp goes on, and back into, and merging with it as the lamp goes off. If one lamp is made to cast a deeper shadow than the other, then the movement of this darker shadow will be particularly striking.

" That is only an optical illusion," I can hear you mutter. Call it that certainly if you will, but remember that as a psychologist you are bound to remain unsatisfied until you have done your best to explain what such a statement means.

Let us in ending this chapter briefly sum up our main contentions : we took the most obvious item of our experience, namely, that our world ' is full of a number of things ' The psychologist, we said, must find in this obvious item of experience a real problem. Having envisaged the problem he must reject an over-simplified solution of it. In groping for a fuller understanding of this phenomenon it became necessary for him to postulate an hypothesis concerning the nature of the relation between body and mind, for our statements concerning the relation of physiological processes to experience are just another name for this. It was

then necessary to test such an hypothesis by means of
a concrete experimental problem, and to show that
the results of this experiment were relevant not only
in our discussion of vision but also within the wider
setting outlined in Chapter I.

Page 25 ff. Cf. W. Köhler, *loc. cit.*, Chap. V.

,,   31 ff. A more detailed exposition of ' Isomorphism ',
i.e. the conception developed here, may be
found in W. Köhler's book, pp. 64 ff.

,,   35 ff. Cf. K. Koffka's *Principles*, Chap. VII, where the
original experiments by Wertheimer, and
the later work, are fully described.

CHAPTER III

OUR EXPERIENCES OF COLOUR AND SOUND

PERHAPS by now you have some idea of what it means
to ' examine the obvious ' : by just opening our eyes
and being conscious in detail of the world we live in,
we have provided ourselves with psychological problems. So far we have discovered that to see ' things '
is a psychological achievement made possible, probably,
by the non-machine-like properties of the organism.
Further, you have been a ' subject ' in an experiment,
the very simplicity of which enabled us to make the
necessary controls ; an experiment which illustrated
our hypothesis about the dynamic qualities of the
organism and showed a psychological experience arising
where it could not have been predicted by the over-
simplified idea of the relation of the physical world to
our experiences.

But there are other aspects of experience, even if I
do nothing more than sit in my chair and look about
the room, which are data for the psychologist, and
which can be treated experimentally by him. One of
the most striking characteristics of the room which I
now see before me, for instance, is its colouring ; and

I might well ask, following my procedure of Chapter II, " Why do I see the cushion as blue, the curtains orange, the walls white and so on ? " The answer would not be " Because they *are* blue, orange, white ", for the things in the physical world have no *colour* in themselves ; it needs our eyes to see colour ; colour, in fact, is another unique achievement of the organism.

In order that this statement may be convincing, and in order that the experiments on colour may be more fully understood, it is necessary for the would-be psychologist to learn something about the physical properties of those light rays which the surfaces we see as coloured reflect and absorb, just as it is necessary for the experimental psychologist himself to take over from the physicist part of his accumulated knowledge and some of his methods of working.

We have spoken already in Chapter II of light rays or light waves which strike our retinæ, but we did not describe these waves themselves, for, strictly speaking, this sort of description belongs to physics ; so let us illustrate by a crude example what these waves are like. If you attach one end of a flexible cord to a door-handle, let us say, you can by moving the other end which you hold in your hand, up and down at a certain speed, make ' waves ' run along the length of the cord between your hand and the end which is fastened. You can make these waves big or small according to the speed with which you move and the energy which you exert. The point of this example is that these waves which move along the rope are caused by different parts of the rope moving up and down, rhythmically, and at different times, and not, of course, by any part of the rope moving along through intervening space. In ' light waves ' the same sort of thing happens ; energy is radiated from the sun and vibrations are set up in the ether which travel with wavelike motions at the incredible speed of 186,326 miles per second ! One way of describing these forms of radiant energy is to indicate their ' wave-length ', the distance between the crests of two successive waves ; we can also describe them in terms of how many times they repeat their characteristic form and motion in one second. The vibrations which concern us now, the light waves which are the physical counterparts of our different experiences of colour, are measured in millionths of a millimetre, and vary in length from about 780 millionths of a millimetre, the ' long ' waves, to 400 millionths of a millimetre, the ' short ' waves. Otherwise expressed, the eye is sensitive to vibrations with wave-lengths within this range.

The eye is sensitive, we said ; but that does not mean that these are the only wavelike vibrations to which we are subjected, or that the eye is the only organ sensitive to certain radiations. Actually we are constantly being bombarded by all sorts of physical energy, in the form of vibrations, travelling through space. We ' see ' the red glow of the fire with our eyes, but we also experience the heat from it all over our bodies. This means that the nerves in our skins react to the rise in temperature brought about by those vibrations from the fire which have a wave-length just longer than the red ones, thus causing us to experience warmth. Then when I speak, ring a bell, drop a book, strike the keys of my typewriter, certain other vibrations, 'sound waves' in this case, also travel off in all directions, but are responded to only by our ears. Finally there is the type of vibration to which no part of my body is sensitive, which I would never know that I had encountered as far as my experience goes, for example the X-ray. When I sit for an X-ray picture, only the photographic plate shows me that these rays really bombarded and passed through me.

After this digression we are almost ready to be psychologists again ; there is, however, one physical demonstration which will help us later. It is possible, physically, to split up ordinary sunlight, which we call ' white light ', into different physical constituents, so that we experience in its place all the colours of the rainbow, or all the colours of the spectrum.   In other words, if you send a beam of white light through a prism of glass, or through a special kind of grating, it will be split up into a number of separate wave-lengths— wave-lengths, that is, which vary from 780 to 400 millionths of a millimetre. This means that for all the colours of the spectrum, red, red-orange, orange, yellow, green, green-blue, blue, blue-violet, there corresponds a specific wave-length, such that, when the particular wave-length 760 millionths of a millimetre strikes my eye, I shall, under normal conditions, see red ; when $575m\mu$ strikes it, yellow and so on.

A prism of glass, then, splits up white light as it passes through it ; the ordinary coloured surfaces which we see around us also do a kind of splitting up, but in this case they reflect back some of the rays, but absorb, or allow to pass into themselves, most of the energy of the others. Thus to appear ' blue ' the cushion reflects back into space the wave-lengths around 400 millionths of a millimetre which we know as the blue ones, and swallows much of the energy of most of the other rays.

This last is a *physical* fact, but its counterpart, the recombining of certain of these components to make white light, gives us our first glimpse of the colour problems of the *psychologist*. If, for instance, I send a beam of blue light from one projection lantern, and a beam of yellow light from a second on to the same spot on a white surface, I ' see ' not a mixture in which blue and yellow can both be distinguished, nor the green which I might have guessed from having mixed paints, but white light, or no colour at all. If I projected a beam of red light from one of my lanterns, and a beam of green light from the other, I should again find the resulting mixture to be white light. In fact, for any pure-coloured beam of light that I choose to project from one of my lanterns I can always find one other colour which, when combined with it, will give me the experience of ' no colour ' instead of the mixture which I might have expected. As far as the eye is concerned then, every colour (every wave-length in the colour range) has some one other colour to which it stands in a peculiar relationship. Whereas red when mixed with blue will give me purple, when mixed with yellow will give orange, yet when mixed with a certain shade of green it yields us the experience of whiteness. This interrelatedness we shall have cause to notice again. While we are speaking of these projection lanterns and coloured beams of light let us notice one more thing which yields rather a surprising experience : if I have three such lanterns, emitting from the one a red beam, from the second a blue, from the third a green, I can, by combining these three lights in different amounts, make any and every other colour, even yellow, which certainly is not experienced as a mixture of any colours at all.

Let us investigate the interconnectedness of certain colours a little more closely. Look at the centre of this little square of yellow, without shifting your eyes from it, for as long as it takes to count twenty.

Now look at the X on the white paper beside it : what do you see ? A square of blue will probably appear as if from nowhere.

Next look at the centre of the somewhat irregular circle of blue for the same length of time.

Is your experience of a more regular circle of yellow ? If the original square had been green you would have seen a red ' after-image , as it is called, if the irregular circle had been red you would have seen a more regular green one, but red will never give me an after-image of yellow or blue, neither will blue give me red or green. Apparently, then, in this matter of the

X

Fig. 3

X

Fig. 4

Fig. 5

after-image, red and green, and blue and yellow demonstrate the same interconnections that they showed in the mixture of coloured lights. Only in this case instead of their showing this connection by cancelling each other out and yielding no coloured experience at all, fixation of the one leads to the spontaneous appearance of the other.

Let us notice in passing another psychological problem : although the square has yielded an after-image that is also a square, the irregular circle became a more regular one. Why ? We must return to this question later.

What about the size of the after-image ? When one ' catches ' it on the original sheet of paper its size is the same as that of the original drawing, but suppose one looks at it on a white surface several feet away, what size will it then be ? Experiment for yourself and see : much bigger. And all intermediate distances will yield intermediate sizes. By measuring distances and sizes you yourself could arrive at an accurate quantitative law concerning the size of that psychological phenomenon, that part of experience, the after-image.

Now let us turn to another problem : look at the coloured plates on the opposite page. These four grey crosses are actually of an identical grey. To convince yourself of this you have only to cover up the coloured areas and see them alone. But when looked at on their backgrounds of black, white, yellow and blue they look quite different in shade and in tone. If the piece of tissue paper covers the whole page these differences in the grey crosses are even more marked : that on the white looks darker than the one on the black, that on the yellow looks darker and at the same time bluer than the one on the blue, which may look tinged with yellow.

Do you see how this problem links up with the one on after-images ? Here are yellow and blue surfaces (and also black and white ones) affecting a grey in terms of each other. Do you also see the kind of question which can be asked so as to yield exact results : for instance, how big can I make the little grey cross and still have the larger coloured surface, on which I place it, take effect, or in psychological terminology, induce this contrast ? Or, can I determine the size of the little grey area which will give the greatest change in its colour ? Or, does the shape of the grey area affect its susceptibility to this change in colour ? Are all shades of grey equally subject to this change, and are all colours equally certain to effect it ? These are psychological problems, for I am investigating something in my experience. Nevertheless, they are situations which can be controlled accurately, and the answers can be in centimetres or millimetres as the case may be, thereby acquiring the validity of numerical results.

If we look at the theoretical side of things for a moment, it becomes increasingly clear that our experiences bear evidence of ' parts affecting other parts '. The same *physical* grey cross gives a different *psycho-*

logical cross when it is alone from what it does when the grey paper is surrounded by an expanse of blue, yellow or black. We know, of course, that nothing has happened to the grey paper itself, and to further convince ourselves we have only to cover up the coloured surroundings and see it alone. When we cover the cross and the background with tissue paper we have another example of this same thing. Here we have, among other things, softened the boundary lines of the cross as a separate entity and have made it merge into its surrounding field. In this case we may say that one part will have a more marked effect on another when the barriers existing between them are diminished.

It is of course quite impossible in a non-technical presentation of any subject to do justice to, or even present at all adequately, the theories which have been evolved to explain discovered facts. Moreover, the purpose of this book is not so much to attempt to answer questions on which even psychologists are not agreed, but rather to indicate the kind of work psychologists do, the kind of problems they find, and how they tackle and develop them. Colour theories, however, stand in rather a special position, being one of the first contributions of the early psychologists. Interestingly enough, even as short a time ago as the last century there were no official experimental psychologists ; the great men whose names are associated with the early development of this subject were physicists, physiologists and philosophers. To give you some idea, however, of just which facts in colour vision a theory tries to unify, cover and explain, we may outline a theory developed by the physiologist Ewald Hering.

We may put the question that confronts all colour theorists in this way : since I must assume a separate organ—the eye for vision ; the ear for sound ; the nose for smell and so on—must I assume a separate part of the eye, a separate kind of nerve cell, or nerve process perhaps, to account for each and every different colour and shade that I see ? Or are there a few fundamentally different and elementary processes, which combine to give the other more complex experiences ? If this be true, which, from the point of view of experience, are the primary colours ? Orange, for example, seems to be both reddish and yellowish : am I therefore to suppose that whatever processes give rise to red, and whatever processes give rise to yellow, must both be active when I see orange ? The same can be said about peacock blue, I can see both green and blue in it : but a pure red, yellow, green or blue, as also black and white, cannot by any stretch of the imagination be seen in terms of each other.

Now the hypothesis that this physiologist made to explain some of the puzzling experiences of colour, took into account the fact that each of these colours is a unique experience ; he also considered of theoretical importance that interconnectedness of red and green, blue and yellow which we pointed out before, and which exists in a similar manner between black and white also. Thus Hering suggested that there might be different pairs of ' photochemical substances ' (chemical substances capable of being activated by light) in the retina of the eye : one pair giving rise to our experience of green and red, another to blue and yellow, and a third to black and white. That physical energy, which we characterize as having a wave-length of about 760 millionths of a millimetre, and which results in our experiencing the colour red, he thought of as ' breaking down ' or disintegrating the photochemical substance in the red-green pair : when the physical energy with a wave-length of 500 millionths of a millimetre acted on this same substance he thought of it as being built up, or added to, with the resulting psychological experience of ' seeing green ' : he thought of a similar breaking down and building up as occurring in the yellow-blue substance.

What happens on this assumption when we see orange or a yellowish-green ? For Hering this was explained by the supposition that ' orange ' light affected both the red-green and the yellow-blue substance, disintegrating both at the same time ; correspondingly, ' yellowish-green ' light breaks down the yellow-blue substance and simultaneously builds up the red-green. To complete the picture Hering assumed that each and every wave-length acted on the black-white substance (breaking it up in every case) in addition to its effect on the other substances.

When you looked just now at that little patch of yellow, a breaking down in the blue-yellow substance occurred in your eye ; consequently when you stopped

looking at it, the substance started to restore its own
balance, to return to a normal state of equilibrium by
building itself up again, and the psychological counterpart of this was your spontaneously seeing a blue
square without anything in the outside world to
cause it.

You will realize how this same idea can explain the
fact that the grey cross looked bluish when placed on
yellow : while the yellow-substance is being ' broken
down ' in the area on the retina corresponding to the
yellow paper, the building up has already begun in the
remaining area, namely, in the area corresponding to
the grey cross, with the result that you experienced
blueness in that area.

We must emphasize again that this theory is not
very fully presented ; it is not the only theory, nor
is it even the most widely accepted one. It serves
to show one thing very clearly, however—that at
certain points the psychologist is driven outside his
own province for his explanations. There is nothing
in our actual experience of the blue after-image
arising from where the yellow square was which tells
us why this happened. Nor does the experience of
' yellowness ' carry with it an explanation of how it
comes about that we have it. Chemistry, however,
can show us that certain substances can be ' broken
down ', others built up in response to certain activating
agents. Physiology can tell us that changes, chemical
changes, undoubtedly occur in the substances within
the minute structures of the eye. The psychologist

observes facts and changes in our world of coloured
experiences, and must ask what type of known natural
process can be used as an explanation.

Before we go further let us review what we have so
far discussed. First, our colour experiences bear a
definite relation to happenings in the physical world ;
the eye is sensitive to a certain range of physical
processes, and gives us different experiences of colour
which, usually, correlate with definite physical wave-
lengths. But we see also that this correlation with
physical happenings is not the whole story. There
are unique psychological facts or experiences which
have no parallels in the physical world. There is the
after-image, that blue square which followed the yellow
one given on the page. That was no figment of your
particular imagination, it is seen by all normal individuals ; yet it has no counterpart in the physical
world. The same is true of such facts as colour and
brightness contrast, which you may remember was the
name given to describe the experienced changes in the
grey cross on the coloured backgrounds. In this case
there are no physical changes to account for the changes
in our experience.

Then we have indicated what is meant by a colour
theory, and have seen again how the psychologist's
work is always twofold : he studies what our experiences actually are, and attempts to find what relationship exists between them and the changes and happenings in the physical world, and to learn from the
physiologist, or to postulate what kind of changes in

the organism would best bridge the gap between these two provinces.

Returning to our discussion we find that we left one psychological fact without an explanation, namely, the after-image of the irregular circle, which had, so to speak, done away with unnecessary irregularities and become more symmetrical. It looks, then, as if that which happens in the organism in this case was somehow similar to those orderly processes which we described in Chapter I, for a regular circle is a simpler and more orderly phenomenon than one with irregularities in it. This apparently trivial occurrence is important not only in giving us another clue to the workings of those physiological processes which accompany our experiences, but in showing that the facts of colour cannot be treated or explained apart from other characteristics of the ' world we see '. Perhaps we should be a little more explicit as to just what happens in this case : in order that an irregular circle be seen as a regular one in the after-image, certain slight humps or bulges on the circumference of the circle which were blue in the original will not, despite all we have said about yellow following blue, give rise to the expected yellow counterparts in the after-image. Or, we could look at it in this way : the areas which are indentations in the white paper in the original now give rise to yellowness in the after-image. This means that the colour of any given point in the after-image is determined by, or is the result of, physiological processes which are interrelated hap-

penings rather than isolated events. In this case
regularity of the circle is achieved despite the fact
that certain small part-processes, if acting entirely
alone, would have resulted in an irregular circle once
more.

Even in such a simple experience, then, as the little
coloured after-image, the question is not only why
does yellow follow blue, but why does the shape
change on one occasion and not on another ?   In
the case of ' contrast ' the question is not only
what will blue, red, yellow and green ' do ' to a
neutral grey, but why does softening the contours
of this grey figure enhance the effect, why are some
shapes more susceptible to the effect than others,
and so on ?

Over and over again the psychologist has been forced
to recognize that it is no use to develop explanations
of isolated parts of his experiences, no use being
satisfied with pointing out too simple connections
between happenings in the physical world and small
pieces of experience. Under ' normal ' conditions,
it is true, certain wave-lengths will give certain experiences of colours, but by changing things in the whole
situation even these particular wave-lengths can give
rise to different experiences, and can even, under
carefully controlled conditions, be made to yield no
experience at all.

This last statement obviously needs elaborating.
We will present it by means of a concrete example,
assuming that you are again serving as a ' subject '

for the experiment or demonstration. You would be sitting about ten feet away from a plain white wall, on which would be a smooth green surface, about two feet square ; in the centre of this surface would be a bright blue star. The blue star would stand out clearly and distinctly from the darker green surface. Then, by simply changing the intensity of the blue light, which was seen by you as the blue star through the star-shaped opening cut in the green surface, I could produce a marked change in your experience. As the blue light became less intense, as it approached a strength equal to that of the darker green, you would begin to lose sight of your star shape, the points would first become blurred, the size of the blue area would decrease until you saw just a small circle, then even this circle would disappear, being submerged in or swallowed up by the green surface.

The explanation of this is not, as I think I hear you suggesting, that we have made the blue so dim that ' you just can't see it ' ; for I have only to make it darker still, only to decrease the intensity of the light still further, for the circle first, and then the star with all its points, to emerge as clearly and distinctly as before. The explanation is that by altering the strength of the blue light we can reach a point where the blue is of exactly equal physiological brightness as the green, and at that one point the blue figure is lost to view. In other words, that particular wave-length which under ordinary circumstances yields the experience of blueness, when surrounded by wave-lengths giving rise to stimulation of equal physiological intensity, no longer gives rise to this experience.

Such an occurrence is of course exactly the converse of that which you ' experienced ' when acting as a subject in the experiment in the last chapter. In that case you saw ' movement ' when there was no physical stimulus to correspond to or cause it. In this case you fail to see blueness although the actual light rays which give rise to blueness on other occasions are still there, striking the retina as before ! If I were to remove the green surface surrounding the star at the time when the star had disappeared, leaving in its place a white surface brighter than the green, you would immediately see your star again, as blue and as star-shaped as it was in the beginning. But under conditions of equal brightness, shape and colour, which are psychological qualities, can be lost. This example is again evidence of the interconnectedness of the processes underlying different aspects of our visual experience.

Although we have only scratched the surface of the interesting things to be discovered by the psychologist in his world of things seen, we must pass on to another phase of our experience, almost equally important, the sounds we hear. By now it will be no surprise to you to be told that, as *sounds*, they cannot exist apart from the ear. People so often ask, ' If a branch falls to the ground from a tree in an isolated and untrodden forest, is there any sound ? ' The answer is, that there are the same physical vibrations travelling through the air as there are when a branch crashes from a tree in your garden, but provided no ears are there for these vibrations to pass into, there is no *sound*.

What are the outstanding characteristics of these sounds which we hear? There are loud sounds and soft sounds, there are noises, there is music with its different tones, there are sounds of speech. In general we can tell where sounds come from. There is also a characteristic of quality in both noises and music. For instance, we never muddle up the noise of cart-wheels with the noise of the ringing telephone. In music, even if the violin and the piano play the same note, equally loud, there is still a difference of quality between them.

Here is a whole new field of investigation for the psychologist. As with sight, it is possible to find certain physical vibrations which are initially respon-sible for certain aspects of our sound experiences. There is a range of vibrations to which the ear is sensitive; between 20 to 30 vibrations per second correspond to the lowest notes which we can hear, somewhere around 30,000 correspond to the highest. The sound waves which give rise to our experience of musical notes are simpler in their structure than those which we experience as noise. When a noise, or a note, is loud it means that the amplitude of its particu-lar wave is greater than it is when we experience a soft sound.

The ear as an organ is too complicated to be described in detail; speaking in very general terms, however, we may say that the ear-drum is made to vibrate in accordance with the sound waves which strike it, and these vibrations pass from one delicate structure to another until they reach a membrane in the inner ear across which numerous fibres of varying lengths are stretched in the manner of strings on a harp. Microscopic hairs on these fibres communicate with the auditory nerve. Just as the eye is the outpost for the brain in the case of sight, sending on its excitations by means of the optic nerve, so the ear receives or picks up this other type of vibration, transmitting its information to headquarters by means of the auditory nerve.

Since we cannot give more than an indication of the psychologist's problems, we choose the question : how is it possible that we know where sounds come from ? Think for a moment of the difference between the eye and the ear. Although we have emphasized very often that the little images on the retinæ are only the beginning of the story of our seeing, there is no difficulty in explaining their orderly arrangement, left right, up down on the retina itself, for, as you can see from the diagram in Fig. 1, the arrangement on the retinæ will be the reverse of the arrangement in space ; what is to the extreme right will be projected to the extreme left and so on. But the ear, structurally at least, shows no way of arranging sounds in accordance with their spatial direction. In so far as there is any structural arrangement which in any way parallels an ordered sequence of vibrations or our ordered experiences it seems to be in terms of pitch rather than direction. By this is meant that the numerous fibres of graded lengths which are stretched across the membrane in the inner ear apparently vibrate individually to an ordered succession of sound waves, and give rise to our experience of notes of different pitch, the shortest fibres corresponding to the highest notes.

But to return to the question of localization : our problem is to find out experimentally how such an achievement is possible. Since one of our first requirements in an experiment is a controlled situation, we begin by limiting the range of experience of our subject. We blindfold him and seat him in a chair. All the way round his chair, at all the points of the figures of the clock, and at several yards' distance, we have fixed buzzers which give a similar sound, and which can be operated by the experimenter from outside the room. Our subject sits facing 12 o'clock. When we are ready to begin we sound the buzzer at, say, 3 o'clock, to the direct right of our subject, who indicates where he heard the sound as coming from ; in this case he has no difficulty in telling that it came from his right. Then we may sound the buzzer at 9 o'clock, and again the subject has no difficulty in locating it to his left. In random order we continue to sound all the various buzzers, until, let us suppose, we have sounded each five times over, the subject in each case recording where he hears the sound as coming from. We must assume also that we have repeated this procedure with a number of subjects and are consequently ready to study their records and see how accurately sound has been 'localized'. As we go through the various records of our subjects it becomes clear that the 12 and 6 o'clock positions, that is, the points directly in front of and behind the subjects, are frequently confused. A sound from the 12 o'clock position is given as 'behind me', one from the 6 o'clock position is given as 'in front of me'. Our records also show a similar confusion between the buzzers at 5 and 1, between 4 and 2, between 7 and 11 and between 8 and 10. In fact, only the sounds from 3 and 9 o'clock, those directly to the right and directly to the left of the subject, are always correctly localized.   Here, then, are our results, but what do they mean ?   Let us look at the correctly localized positions first ; what have they in common which distinguishes them from the others ?

It can be seen from the diagram that the buzzer at 3 is further away from the right ear than it is from the left ; the converse is true for the 9 o'clock position and the left ear. Concerning 12 and 6, positions frequently confused, we find that the distance from both to both ears is equal : whereas that member of each of the other pairs of positions which have been confused one with the other, is nearer to one ear than the other by the same amount.

But you will be saying, how does this help us ? Let us make an hypothesis : since sound waves are comparatively slow moving, and since the two ears are about six inches apart, it must happen that the sound waves coming from the right will reach the

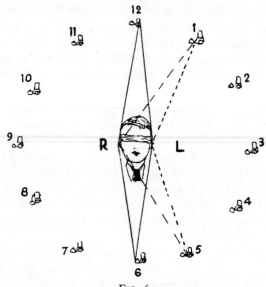

Fig. 6.

——— paths equal to both ears from both sounds.
- - - - paths from sounds to right ear, equal to each other and both
          longer than the corresponding left paths.
. . . . paths from sounds to left ear.

right ear before these same sound waves reach the left ear. Might it not be that we recognize a sound as coming from the direction of the ear which first receives the sound wave, with the angle at which the sound appears to come from depending on, and varying with, the amount of the time difference?

How shall we test such an hypothesis? If it were correct, it ought to be possible to make a sound, which actually originates from the right of the subject, appear to be coming from his left if we so arranged it that the sound waves reached his left ear first! The simplest way of achieving this is by putting into each ear a horn which bends back over the head and

FIG. 7.

faces the opposite direction. Thus a sound from the right reaches the left ear first, since the route to be travelled to the right ear involves the extra distance. The reverse is true for a sound originating from the left.

In this experiment we find that our hypothesis is confirmed; our blindfolded subject hears the sound as coming, not from its real direction, but from the opposite.

Another way of testing our hypothesis would be to furnish our subject with ear pieces to which are attached metal tubes with trombone-like extensions, so that by lengthening either tube the path to be travelled by the sound waves to either ear can also be lengthened. Let us suppose that the tube is originally longer on the subject's right-hand side ; then if a sound actually in the middle (at X) is heard as coming from the left, we have confirmed our theory. And

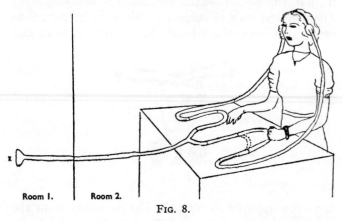

Room I.　　Room 2.

FIG. 8.

Dotted lines indicate position of trombone before it has been pulled out, i.e. when pathways to both ears are equal.

we can even go a step further, for we can ask the subject himself to lengthen the tube attached to his left ear by extending the trombone as indicated by the dotted lines in the figure, and if in this case the sound appears to travel back to the centre as this second tube is pulled to the same length as the first, and to travel to the right as it is made longer, then we can be reasonably sure that our determining factor has been this difference in time with which the sound reached each ear : no time difference being the ' signal ' for ' straight ahead ' and the varying angles to the right or left depending on the varying time differences.

As a matter of fact, in an experimental situation exactly this happens.

In the experiments so far mentioned the subject has been blindfolded : what will happen, we may now ask, if the blindfold is removed and the conflicting evidence of eyes and ears presented ?   If the experiment with the horns bent over the head is made at an open window, what will happen if a car is now seen as approaching from the left while the ear horns continue to ' give it ' as coming from the right ?   In such a case the evidence of the eyes overcomes the evidence of the ears, and the car is heard, as it is seen, to approach from the left.

A common example of this triumph of ' eye ' over ' ear ' is given in the talkies. We hear the voices as coming from the actors whose lips we see moving and to whom the speech ' belongs '. Actually all sounds are emitted from the same loud-speaker, located high in the centre of the screen. These facts tell us something important : not only is there an interaction between different parts of our world of sight as we have pointed out, not only, as could also have been shown, do different aspects of our world of sound influence each other, but there is also an interaction between these two provinces of experiences. Our total experience bears evidence that the brain has in some way united the processes arising from the stimulation of separate sense organs.

We have attempted in this chapter to extend the psychologist's province a little further, for your inspection.   In ordinary life we use our experience of colours and sounds so much to help us to find out things about the world itself, that we are apt to forget, or never even to think of the fact that these same experiences in themselves are also a rich field for systematic investigation.

Page 51 ff. For a general discussion of Colour Theories
see C. Ladd-Franklin, *Colour and Colour
Theories*. London and New York, 1928.
„ 58.   Cf. K. Koffka's discussion of the Liebmann
effect, *loc. cit.*, pp. 126 f.
„ 65.   The experiment with the crossed earphones
was performed by P. T. Young, and is re-
ferred to in many modern text-books of
psychology ; cf. R. H. Wheeler, *The Science
of Psychology*. New York.

CHAPTER IV

So far, in order to emphasize how much of psychology is an examination of those experiences which we take completely for granted, we have chosen to discuss those problems which can be discovered by our doing nothing more than sitting in a chair and becoming more explicitly conscious of the characteristics of our own rooms. We have discussed, that is, a few of the innumerable problems which can arise from how the world looks to us, and how the world sounds to us.

But, as by this time I can hear you saying, we don't sit in a chair and just look, or just hear all our lives : we do things, move about, eat our meals, talk to other people, feel happy, despondent, excited, think over things, read books, and remember or forget what we have read ; moreover, we are members of different and important groups, our families, our communities, our countries. Exactly, and you have every right to demand from experimental psychology the same consideration and isolation of the problems involved here, that were found to be given to those aspects of experience which we have already discussed. But we started our discussion of experimental psychology with these particular problems for several reasons, which it may help us to review before we go further.

You remember that the psychologist found himself between the devil and the deep sea with regard to criticisms from scientist and layman. On the one hand he was criticized because, to a scientific outsider, it seemed that human life was far too complex ever to be submitted to the stringent demands of science's controlled and repeatable experiments. On the other hand, the psychologist had to deal with the criticism of those who felt that psychology was just dry stuff, neglecting the essence of what is human in behaviour.

We have tried in the preceding pages to show that neither criticism is really justified : at the present stage of psychological theory and technique, it is possible to maintain controlled experimental conditions with some problems, and yet it is also possible to understand these somewhat specific problems so that they do relate to more general and vital ones.

But we have to admit at this point that the more complex the activity which we investigate becomes, the less we are able to comply with the strict demands of science. Suppose that I am working on the after-image, and wish to make sure, in a way that will satisfy a scientist, that a green after-image follows the presentation of a red figure. I might take as many as 10,000 people, and have them look at the red figure and, apart from a possible colour-blind individual, I should find that they all experienced the green after-image.   I could conduct the experiment so that they all looked at the same red figure, in the same light, for the same length of time.   An important fact for science would be that this 'experiment' could be repeated by anyone else, because he could repeat all the conditions exactly.   Now amongst these 10,000 people there might be old and young, men and women, rich and poor, coloured and white, happy or unhappy people.   It would be quite unnecessary to control these conditions ; they would be irrelevant because what I am investigating is what the normal eye sees in this connection, and the normal eye is not affected by these conditions, any more than a chemical solution in a test-tube would be affected by the size of the table on which the test-tube was standing.

But suppose I take another problem, a problem more like those which you originally felt psychology ought to deal with : why do I get angry if someone incessantly and unnecessarily interrupts me during important work ?   That is going to be more difficult. In the first place, what is ' anger ' ?   And even granted that I could explain what is meant by anger as an activity of the organism, to produce anger in a laboratory under controlled conditions is more difficult than producing a red figure to be looked at.   What exactly ought I to control here ?   Must I, in order to have the necessary relevant material, know all the things which my subject has ever been angry about, if, or why, he is particularly touchy that morning, if he has had bad news, if he has made a resolution not to

let certain things annoy him? You can see where
it begins to be difficult to determine, and to collect,
all the relevant data. Or suppose that I want to
investigate a particular relationship of several people
in a group; just when could I ever say that I knew
enough about all of them so that I should be able
to control and repeat an experimental situation? As
personalities, as members of that group, they are
constantly changing, new influences are playing on
them; how can I keep pace with them so as to feel
that I control the situation?

It is for reasons of this kind that psychology is
forced to make a beginning where it can conduct its
experiments with complete scientific strictness, admit-
ting that there are only certain realms of behaviour
for which it is equipped to deal in this way at the
present time. Nevertheless, there is experimental
work going on at the more complex level, and after
this digression, we may again take up your objection
that we not only see and hear, but that we also *do*
things.

As human beings we do so many things that our
first task, as psychologists, is to make some sort of
distinction between different kinds, or types, of actions.
For instance, I ' do something ' when I sneeze, and I
do something when I sit for an hour trying to solve
a mathematical problem, but no one would think of
these activities as being very similar. I do something
when I eat, or when I step out of the way quickly
to avoid being bumped into; I do something different

when I sit down in a chair after deciding to do so rather than go to the piano and play, from what I do when I sit down to relax.

When I sneeze, draw back my hand from a hot surface, blink at a bright light, or breathe, there is very little of myself involved. It is as if my body took charge of such actions almost entirely, except on those occasions when ' I ' decide to enter the arena in a particularly forceful manner. But even when I enter I can only modify the procedure, I cannot really alter or dispense with it completely. I can, with difficulty, stop my sneezing—sometimes. I can stop my breathing—for a very short space of time. Its rate, it is true, will depend on how excited ' I ' am, but with the exception of such things we might characterize this type of action as one about which ' you ' or ' I ' not only have very little to say, but which we never have had to learn how to do.

If this ' unlearned ' aspect of behaviour is to be a basis of classification, we may ask, how about eating ? Don't babies know how to suck without being taught, and does not our eating now take place without our having to think about how we should do it ? Yes, and no, we must answer : eating is obviously more like sneezing than it is like solving a mathematical problem, but there are differences which would obscure the issue for us if we neglected to point them out. For instance, compared with blinking, eating is a complex phenomenon. Any time my eye is touched or threatened, or a bright light is directed into it, I

will blink ; but, in general, I will eat only when I am
hungry ; I will not sit down to a second meal immediately after completing a first. On the other hand,
I may be very hungry and yet not touch the food on
the table before me ; good manners may prohibit it
until a belated guest arrives. Or I may be unwilling
to eat and yet force myself to, for other, equally
compelling social reasons. There is also more of ' me '
involved in eating than in blinking, in that there are
definite things that I dislike, which my neighbour
may relish, whereas we both will blink uniformly
at the light, and sneeze willy-nilly when we have
colds. It is true that we do not have to think how
to eat : but we had to learn, and even if sucking is
one of the baby's first amazing achievements, his
technique is also subject to the rule of practice-makes-
perfect. Into this category we may also put walking,
and our continuous and successful adaptation to the
physical environment in the sense that we do not
as a rule collide with the furniture, or trip over rugs,
and yet do not have to think about this manœuvring.

Let us make a third category. You will have noticed
that in both the preceding groups of actions, particularly in the first, there was an automatic element.
In the group now in question what is automatic is our
own rather than characteristic of the whole race.
I may continually fold my hands in a certain manner,
while you may always be saying certain words, or
ending your sentences with a particular inflection,
or sitting down with your legs crossed in a ' char-

acteristic' manner. These actions may be done invariably and automatically by you or me, but they are not uniform to all of us in the sense that sneezing and blinking or eating and walking are.

We shall have to have another distinct category for actions that are the result of careful deliberation and choice. Here there will be almost no uniformity or automatic character, while more and more of 'myself' or 'yourself' will be involved. Within this group the complexity of the action may vary greatly, as may also the amount of deliberation which precedes. I may decide to go out just because the sun is shining, and embody this decision in one action ; but I may also decide to direct all my energies to studying medicine rather than law, thereby determining thousands and thousands of future actions.

We may distinguish one more type of action, namely, those which involve solving a problem. If I get a flat tyre in a crowded thoroughfare my choice of actions may lie between sitting and waiting for help, or attempting to remedy the situation myself. Once I have decided to act in the latter way, I am confronted with the problem of getting the old tyre off and the new one on, and all my doings will be directed towards this specific end. The actual demands of this limited situation will determine entirely what movements I shall make, and I shall perform actions, which in and of themselves without relation to this problem would be quite meaningless.

You will notice that in sorting out some of the

things which we do, in order to make our problems a
little clearer, we have refrained from naming each
type of action at the outset ; this is because names
have a dangerous tendency to become explanations
in and of themselves, instead of remaining convenient
labels.   Provided we are alive to this danger, however,
it may help us to classify our first group as *reflex
actions*, the second as being the result of *instinctive
tendencies*, the third as being *habits*, the fourth and
fifth as being *intelligent actions*, involving deliberate
choice and the solving of problems.

In so far as possible it is our aim in these chapters,
not merely to present a summary of experimental
work, but to see what these experiments mean in a
wider setting.   Naturally this is not always possible ;
no science, psychology least of all, has progressed in
such a way that at any given time the full significance
of all its investigations is apparent.   However, in
beginning a new topic, the action of the organism, or
its behaviour, it is well to have certain general questions in mind.   A very natural one is : ' Is man a
machine ? '   For we may say, granted that we have
been able to show evidence to the contrary in the
preceding chapters, how will our assumptions fare in
this new field ?

In the remainder of this chapter we shall concern
ourselves with the first two types of action which
we spoke of, the reflexes and instinctive behaviour.
Here our theoretical issue concerns the claims of one
school of psychologist that this type of automatic

and mechanical action is sufficient to explain all our behaviour, however complex. What factors suggest such an interpretation, and what kinds of experiments are performed to substantiate it ?

I am sure that no one of you has escaped hearing of these reflexes, and perhaps even of ' conditioned ' reflexes in your newspaper and novel reading during the last years. It may be well, however, to describe the actual nervous structure and nerve action which this term designates and implies. What happens is something like this : excitation, started on the surface of the body, say by the prick of a pin on one small spot, is communicated by one nerve, to one central cell (which, incidentally, is in the spinal cord and not in the brain) and from there by one other nerve to the muscle of the hand, which, on receiving the stimulation contracts, thus drawing the hand away from the pin. This simple structure of cells in the skin, nerves, central cell and muscle is called a reflex arc ; and its seemingly simple one-track functioning gives rise to the reflex action of the withdrawing from the painful situation.

In order to bring out the essential characteristics of both the reflex arc and reflex action we chose as our example one of the simplest possible reflexes in which a minimum number of bodily parts may be involved : but there are other reflexes which are more complicated, as for example, when a new-born baby cries when it is hungry. Now in order that the child cry, several bodily organs must be brought into play, not only one set of muscles as in the previous case, but essentially the same pattern of nervous activity exists. The 'messages' sent from the sensitive organs are transmitted by a direct route to those organs responsible for crying.

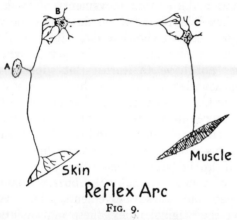

Reflex Arc

FIG. 9.

A is the cell body of the sensory nerve, C that of the motor nerve, and B that of a connecting nerve not mentioned in the text, for even this diagrammatic sketch is slightly more complicated than the arc described on p. 78.

The question is still open, however, as to how much of our entire behaviour is really explicable in this way. For you will object, I imagine, that not all our actions are of this kind, as simple as the withdrawing of the hand from the prick of a pin or the automatic crying and moving of a hungry or startled baby. But the psychologist who believes in this type of action as fundamental, is ready for you on that point. That is where the 'conditioned reflex' comes in as his most valuable explanatory concept, and as we explain this term we may show the experimenter at work.

Let us first make a general explanation of what this conditioning means : a new-born baby will open its mouth and make certain movements of its lips and tongue when it is taking its food. These movements since they occur on the first day after birth can be considered an original reflex, an action which the child does not have to learn. But suppose that a buzzer is sounded before the child is permitted to take his milk, and just after he has begun to take it, and this procedure is repeated for a number of days at feeding times, it will be found that finally the child will open his mouth and make these lip and tongue movements at the buzzer alone, whenever it is sounded, although of course originally the buzzer would never have called out these movements. This type of change in the original reflex, these movements made in a situation different from the normal one, is called the 'conditioning' of the reflex. And it is because such transference can be made to occur, not only with these particular movements but with any of the original reflexes, and not only with babies but with adults and animals as well, that some psychologists make the claim that all seemingly complex actions are in fact built up out of the variations on the original reflexes with which we are endowed.

Let us describe an experiment of this kind in greater detail, one in which a dog is the experimental 'sub-

ject ' and the reflex which is investigated is the salivary
one. The salivary glands, as you know, are those
responsible for making our mouths water at the taste
and smell of good food. This mouth-watering is of
course a reflex action ; we cannot in any way control
it, while certain objects only will bring it about. It is
possible to attach a tube in the dog's mouth so that
the saliva instead of being swallowed, is drained
away and its amount can be accurately measured
drop by drop. The dog is put on a table, the tube
attached, and the food shown to him : when his
mouth waters this is indicated by the saliva drained
off by the thin tube. If we then show him his food
and sound a bell simultaneously, we shall find after
about 60 such repetitions that the dog's mouth will
water even when the bell is sounded alone and no
food is shown. In other words, the reflex has become
conditioned, having now become attached to a situation
other than that to which it originally belonged.

This procedure may be varied so that with the
sight of food a note on a tuning fork, say middle C,
may be sounded, and such repetitions again continued
until the dog's mouth waters for the note when it is
unaccompanied by the sight and smell of food. Now
in this case we might ask two questions : what does
the dog really respond to when his mouth waters
to the note alone ? does he really hear a *note*, the note
C, and would he be able to discriminate this note from
some other note, responding to the one he had been
practising with, and not to the other ? And secondly,

provided our first question was answered in the affirma-
tive, how accurate is his ability to distinguish notes?

Since we can never ask the dog if he hears the
difference between two notes, you will realize that this
experimental procedure provides us with a way of
arriving at such an answer which would otherwise be
beyond our power. If, for instance, the dog heard
no difference between middle C and E or G then he
could never be trained to respond to one rather than
the other, his mouth would water equally when G
was sounded even if he had been trained exclusively
with the note C. At first, it is true, just this appears
to be the case, for in the words of one experimenter
" the most diverse tones and noises are effective ",
that is, the dog's mouth will water even to noises
and notes other than those used in his training;
but it is not long before he is further trained so as
to respond only to the one note, so that we are entitled
to say that he does hear something which distinguishes
this particular note from others. As for his power
of discrimination, that is quite remarkable; some
dogs can actually be trained to discriminate between
sounds which are only one-eighth of a tone apart.
Such exacting experiments, however, proved to be a
strain on the animal, rendering him nervous and
' hysterical '.

Turning now to human adult subjects we may mention an experiment which furnishes important evidence
for the theory under discussion. It has been found
that one cannot only make a reflex follow on some

neutral stimulus rather than its own, but can make
it follow the stimulus for some other reflex, and at
times can, apparently, even do away with this other
reflex itself. For example : normally the pupils of
the eyes were found to dilate automatically when a
bell was sounded, but under experimental conditions
(i.e. by flashing a bright light into the eye simultaneously with the sounding of the bell) the opposite effect,
the contracting of the pupils, could be brought about
when the bell was again sounded alone. At the end
of the experiment, then, the pupils were contracting
to the sound of the bell although originally they had
been dilating.

The same experimenter who noted this brought
about the contraction of the pupils to several other
stimuli in addition to the bell, for instance, to the
speaking of nonsense syllables by the experimenter, to
the subject's own whispered command of ' contract ',
and finally even to his ' thinking ' the words of command. This last is of great importance in understanding the claims of the psychologist who pins his
faith in this mechanism as fundamental to all actions ;
for such an experiment, in the words of a supporter,
" probably lays bare the essential mechanism of what
has been known to the classical psychologist " (not to
mention the ' man in the street ') " as voluntary action
or will ". In other words, when we ' will ' ourselves
to do something we believe we are acting as free
individuals, but in reality, according to such a view,
nothing more is happening than a conditioned reflex

taking place in our organism. ' Thought ' becomes part of the conditioned reflex mechanism, for ' thought ' is nothing more than certain muscular contractions, involved originally in whispering the command, and now suppressed. According to these psychologists then it is by such mechanisms as those we have described that our whole repertoire of actions expands and multiplies. Because of the innumerable possible combinations of the various reflexes with happenings, or stimuli, in the outside world, they feel that no other *type* of explanation is necessary, even for such a complex action as thinking.

While, undoubtedly, these results can be achieved experimentally the question still remains as to whether they are so fundamental that they should be taken as the explanation of all kinds of actions. It is clear, moreover, from our general discussions, that such a mechanical philosophy is not one we have advanced in these chapters ; however, even if we do not accept these principles we must be prepared to learn from these experiments. They have shown us, for example, that animals and children can be very useful ' subjects ' even though we cannot draw upon their experience and testimony to help us in formulating our conclusions. In fact, we can go farther and say that the psychologist can and should study behaviour in many cases without resorting to the subject's own interpretation of what he did or what happened to him. This is an important step towards removing one of the objections raised against psychology by our scientific critic; for, you will remember, science demands that any scientist must be able to repeat an experiment; that whatever is observed must be generally available, and must not be the experience of one individual alone. And of course, consciousness, your consciousness, my consciousness, is completely ' private ', and in no sense can it be observed by other scientists. Thus these experiments have shown that from the observable behaviour of an animal, child, or adult, there is much to be learned, and because of this emphasis on behaviour as opposed to consciousness or experience, this school of thought has been called Behaviourism, a name which you may have come across in texts other than psychological.

We must now mention briefly that other type of action which, in the case of animals at least, is ' ready made ' at birth—such an action as the building of its nest by the robin in the particular ' robin fashion ', the burying of nuts by the young squirrel, the pouncing on small moving objects of the kitten, and so on. That such actions are simply sequences or chains of reflexes, each set off by the preceding one, is the obvious claim of the Behaviourist, who is particularly on his guard against any suggestion of attributing consciousness to the animal's performance when such a performance can be explained without it. While we must beware, it is true, of projecting our own ways of doing things into the animal world, nonetheless it is possible, using our non-mechanical concepts, to build up an explanation of instinctive action in other than purely automatic and mechanical terms. This we shall attempt to do at the end of the chapter.

Much important work on instinctive behaviour has been done through observation of animals and insects in natural conditions rather than by experimentation proper, books have been written on the wasp and ant, for example, showing the amazingly complicated yet relatively uniform behaviour of these insects generation after generation. But there is another aspect of the concept of instinct, over and above these actions which ' belong ' to the organism and which are achieved without imitation or practice, and that is the drive, power or energy behind these actions such that they will be completed in spite of difficulties, either natural or experimentally introduced. We may illustrate experimental work on these instinctive drives by asking the question " Which is the stronger of two such drives, that towards satisfying the animal's hunger or that of sex ? " Or, in the manner of the experimenter, " How much of an obstacle will be needed to thwart each of these drives respectively ? "

One pre-requisite for such an experiment would be an animal, a rat let us say, whose immediate previous existence had been controlled, that is, one that we know to be hungry and sexually excited. We may then put this animal in a box with two alternative exits, one leading him to a female rat, the other to food. We would put him in time and time again, removing him before he could satisfy either of these instinctive drives. We would answer our question in terms of the number of times that he chose one route rather than the other.

Or we could put the rat on a small platform, on another part of which is either food, or a female rat in plain view, but to reach either of these objectives he must cross a mesh of wire from which he would receive an electric shock which can be made stronger and stronger. Here we can measure the amount of current necessary to deter him from reaching either the food or the female rat. Or we could adopt the method of counting the number of times, during a given interval, that he will cross the wire to reach either the food or the female, despite the shock he receives. Experiments of this kind have shown that the maternal drive appears to be the strongest, followed in order by thirst, hunger, sex, and curiosity.

A second type of experiment which utilizes the animal's instinctive drives, does so to throw light on the question of animal learning. Most of these experiments involve a maze, at the entrance of which the rat is placed, and in which he is left to find the food in the centre or further end. The rat is put in such a maze over and over again until he learns it so completely that he runs straight to the food without turning down any of the blind alleys. All sorts of questions concerning this learning arise, how many trials the rat will need before he can run the maze without fault, what kind of errors he will make, and so on ; in short, how does a rat learn ? What concerns us now is the relation of certain instinctive drives to this process of learning. Does a rat, driven by acute hunger, learn more rapidly than one that is less hungry ? Yes, and this even if the very hungry rats are not rewarded with food at the end of the maze. If the rat is rewarded with food immediately does that affect his subsequent learning ? Yes, he learns faster if food is presented immediately after the run than he does if it is given after a delay of some minutes. Does the kind of food that his hunger is appeased with affect his learning ? Yes, certain foods are apparently more desired and more satisfying than others, giving rise to better performances in their attainment. Will a thirsty rat, on finding water, do better than this same rat, who, though thirsty, has found food? Yes, poor performances following the finding of food as the reward will improve rapidly when water is found in its stead. Will a female rat, trying to find her litter in order to feed them, do better than this same rat when she no longer needs to feed them ? Yes, when the need to nurse has diminished, the rat's accuracy and speed in threading the maze has diminished too.

Needless to say the answers to these questions do not rest on the performance of one rat, but on the average performance of many. Moreover, we must remember that not all questions that are asked, or the conclusions that are reached after much careful and accurate work, are equally valuable ; for, even when we know a lot of detailed facts about such instinctive drives, we have not necessarily understood these facts in the light of wider and more significant problems.

But, you will ask, how do we know that a problem *is* significant ? Perhaps we do not : but at least the wider setting which we have chosen for this book, requires that we say something more constructive about these ways of behaving, the simple reflex and the instinctive actions, beyond denouncing a mechanical explanation of them, and enumerating experimental problems. What have we then to offer to supersede the strictly mechanical approach ? A not illogical suggestion, and one in line with our general approach, would be that these seemingly automatic actions, reflexes and instincts, instead of serving as the mechanical standard to which all other actions have to be reduced, might themselves be shown, by further investigation, to exhibit characteristics of freedom and spontaneity.

Let us attempt such an alternative in regard to instinctive behaviour : when an animal is hungry and ' instinctively seeks food ', such hunger means that its total bodily system is under stress, owing to the lack of certain nutritive chemical components. Now a great many different actions may appease hunger, that is, bring about the restoration of the physical balance. These actions when analysed minutely would probably vary considerably from occasion to occasion. In other words the same stimulus, ' hunger ', bringing about finally the same end-result of satisfaction, does *not* set off the same inevitable series of reflex movements as a mechanical theory must demand : what it sets off are some actions relevant to relieving the peculiar plight of the organism, namely hunger. The young bird seeking food, for example, may do something quite different when he pecks at grubs from under a stone, from what he does when he pulls a long worm out of the ground.

Now in Chapter I we noticed that even systems in the physical world restored their balance ' spontaneously ' in ways indicating that they possessed more than one degree of freedom ; all we are doing now is making a similar assumption for what goes on in the body of the animal during instinctive behaviour. We are claiming, in short, that we need not attribute to the bird a conscious insight into its state of hunger when it relieves this hunger in a relevant way, but at the same time we are rendering equally unnecessary a purely automatic interpretation, by postulating a nervous system capable of relieving itself from a state of tension in a variety of ways, guided by the circumstances of the moment.

And reflex action itself ?   We will content ourselves here with one observation : a reflex action is an occurrence in which, as nearly as possible, one single part of the organism operates by itself ; in other words, it is not the organism as a totality, a system, a whole, that is involved. It is therefore perfectly possible that such a unit, such a relatively isolated part, may to all intents and purposes be automatic in its limited action. But as a matter of fact even this isolation and limited action has, for purposes of simplification, and because it constitutes a convenient tool of thought, been over-emphasized. "Actually," as an eminent neurologist has recently put it, "simple reflexes are always under the influence of larger patterns of behaviour only being emancipated by experiment or disease." Elsewhere this same author states that, "By imagining this simple mechanism (the reflex arc), multiplied and complicated thousands of times, one gets a mechanistic idea of how the brain works. But like all mechanistic views, the scheme is inadequate and not true to life ; for correlated work on embryology and physiology shows that quite complex forms of behaviour are laid down in the anatomy of the spinal cord", actions which, when the time comes, appear in their totality, showing that they are not "built up by compounding simple reflexes". This evidence, coming as it does not from psychologists, but from workers whose speciality is a study of the nervous system, is an interesting added corroboration of the views we have been advancing.

Pavlov's *Lectures on Conditioned Reflexes* (London), and C. L. Hull's article on Learning in the *Handbook of General Experimental Psychology*, ed. C. Murchinson (Worcester, Mass.), are relevant as general reading for this chapter. As a contrast to the views expressed in these works the reader will find W. McDougall's *Energies of Man* (London) of interest.

Page 82. Cf. Anrep, ' Pitch Discrimination in the Dog,' *Journal of Physiology*, Vol. 53.
,,   83. Cf. C. L. Hull, *loc. cit.*, p. 417.
,,   86. Cf. such books as W. M. Wheeler's *The Social Insects*. London and New York, 1928.
,,   86 f. Cf. C. J. Warden, *Animal Motivation* (New York and London) and *Outline of Comparative Psychology* (London).
,,   87 f. Cf. E. C. Tolman, *Purposive Behaviour in Animals and Men*. New York, 1932.
,,   91. Cf. Stanley Cobb, *A Preface to Nervous Disease*, p. 16. New York, 1936.

CHAPTER V

EMERGENCE OF MORE COMPLEX BEHAVIOUR

In the last chapter we discussed only two of the several types of action into which, for convenience, we had classified our general behaviour. We spoke of reflex action and the instinctive actions of animals together because they had one outstanding feature in common, namely, that the organism is somehow equipped with them in a more or less perfect form at birth, that they do not need to be learned. But if we think over our own total behaviour, or, from the standpoint taken in these chapters, that of many animals as well, it becomes evident that such actions in and of themselves constitute a very small part of our active lives. For we must admit that most of the things we do, we have first to learn before they are part of our repertoire. True, we may have built on certain innate capacities, but in the main our intelligent and relevant ways of acting are not ready-made, but are the result of continual modification through trial, error, insight and experience. The study of this achieving, modifying and changing of behaviour, in view of the situation with which we are confronted, is the next general topic on which we must embark in order to give a more complete picture of the psychologist at work.

Let us begin by disentangling some of the problems related to learning and by stretching this concept beyond its schoolroom connotation, for we are apt perhaps in ordinary usage to give a somewhat restricted meaning to the term, and to think of it as referring to ' learning by heart ' only.

We shall try and distinguish three aspects of learning and at the same time utilize these to show three different kinds of experimental procedure, work with animals, children and adults. We shall begin with the learning of something for the first time, with that psychologically interesting moment when a relevant and intelligent action, never before performed, appears in the behavioural repertoire.

We have chosen for our subjects in the experiment some chimpanzees ; and this for several reasons. First, because in general it is easier to put an adult animal into a completely new situation than it is to find such a situation for a human being. Secondly, because after what has been said in Chapter IV the question may have arisen in your mind as to whether psychologists consider animals fit subjects only for those ' lower ' or more primitive ways of behaving, even if they did not all go so far as to attribute purely automatic actions to them. Periodically one sees the question raised in the newspapers as to whether or not animals have intelligence. Someone writes a letter claiming that his dog or cat exhibited this or that reasonable quality, and as likely as not some scientifically minded person, who has no dog or cat, refutes them. Psychologists have indulged in such arguments themselves, and there have been experiments performed which seemed to show that all the animal was really capable of was a series of random movements, one of which, by accident, was finally successful in ' achieving ' the solution to the problem. To those of you who have animals such a suggestion may not seem very convincing, and there is not space here to give these experiments or arguments in full ; suffice it to say that the fault in many cases seems to have lain with the experimenter for giving the animal a problem which it was actually impossible for it to solve intelligently. Our third reason, therefore, for choosing these particular experiments with the chimpanzees is that they were devised so as to afford the animal every chance of solving his problem intelligently and of achieving a new and relevant action which he had not performed before.

If you wish to make the further acquaintance of several delightful chimpanzees you would do well to read the book from which these passages are taken ; for the moment we must be satisfied with somewhat brief descriptions. The general question asked in these experiments was, What can the chimpanzee achieve in order to obtain food placed in a difficult position, such food being available, however, provided certain intelligent steps are taken ?   Let us introduce our first ' subject ' : Koko.

Koko, judged to be about three years of age, was a type of chimpanzee not uncommonly met with : above his drum taut stomach a pretty face with a tidy parting, a pointed chin, and prominent eyes which seemed always discontentedly asking for something, giving the little fellow a native expression of sauciness. A large part of his existence was, in fact, spent in a kind of chronic indignation, either because there was not enough to eat or because the children dared to come near him, or because someone, who had just been with him, dared to go away again, or finally, because he did not remember to-day what he had done in a similar test yesterday.

Koko on this occasion is faced with the problem of obtaining a banana placed beyond the reach of his arm, but available provided a stick is used to pull it nearer. Let us watch this occurrence in imagination :

On the second day after his arrival (at the ape station in Teneriffe where these experiments were made) Koko was, as usual, fastened to a tree with a collar and chain. A thin stick was secretly pushed into his reach ; he did not notice it at first, then he gnawed at it for a minute. When an hour had elapsed, a banana was laid upon the ground, outside the circle of which his chain formed a radius, and also beyond his reach. After some useless attempts to grasp it with his hand, Koko suddenly seized the stick, which lay about one metre behind him, gazed at his objective, then again let fall the stick. He then made vigorous efforts to grasp the objective with his foot, which could reach farther than his hand . . . then he suddenly took the stick again, and drew the objective towards himself, though very clumsily.

Let us now watch Nueva, another of the chimpanzees, at the same task :

> Nueva was tested three days after her arrival. She had not yet made the acquaintance of the other animals but remained isolated in her cage. A little stick is introduced into her cage ; she scrapes the ground with it, pushes the banana skins together into a heap, and then carelessly drops the stick at a distance of about three-quarters of a metre from the bars. Ten minutes later, fruit is placed outside the cage beyond her reach. She grasps at it, vainly of course, and then begins the characteristic complaint of the chimpanzee : she thrusts both lips . . . especially the lower . . . forward, for a couple of inches, gazes imploringly at the observer, utters whimpering sounds and finally flings herself on the ground on her back . . . a gesture most eloquent of despair which may be observed on other occasions as well. Thus between lamentations and entreaties, some time passes, until . . . about seven minutes after the fruit has been exhibited to her . . . she suddenly casts a look at the stick, ceases her moaning, seizes the stick, stretches it out of the cage, and succeeds though somewhat clumsily in drawing the banana within arm's length.

Let us now look in on a situation which has been made more difficult, the food this time being placed so far from the bars that even the additional length of a stick cannot reach it. A second stick, however, is left in the cage, which can be fitted into a hole in the top of the first, thus making an implement sufficiently long so that the fruit may be reached : but can the chimpanzee achieve this intelligent solution ?

Here is Sultan faced with this problem after several previous attempts :

> Sultan first of all squats indifferently on the box, which has been left standing a little back from the railings ; then he gets up, picks up the two sticks, sits down again on the box and plays carelessly with them. While doing this, it happens that he finds himself holding one rod in either hand in such a way that they lie in a straight line ; he pushes the thinner one a little way into the opening of the thicker, jumps up and is already on the run towards the railing to which he has up to now half turned his back and begins to draw a banana towards him with the double stick.

Chimpanzees, therefore, are capable of solving this problem : they are able to employ a tool to bridge a gap, and even to make a tool in order to do so. Moreover, so completely was this problem mastered, so unmistakably was this 'idea' of something-to-make-the-arm-longer learned, that when a stick was not available the animals would seize on makeshifts, would break off the branch of a tree, or pull a bar out of an old shoe scraper, would manipulate straw until it yielded some sort of an implement, or even fetch an old bed-cover to be used in angling for the distant food.

Another problem which was given to the chimpanzees, and one which caused some of them much difficulty, was that of moving obstacles away from the bars in order that the food might be reached. If a box was put against the bars of the cage, blocking the opening through which the food could be secured,

what would the animal do ? Here is Sultan, one of
the cleverest apes, in this situation :

> Sultan's first actions were unclear : he seated himself
> on the box and tried vainly to reach the objective with
> the stick. Sometimes he shook the box a little. Finally
> he lost hold of the stick which fell outside the bars, and
> no other was available. Then Sultan actually took
> hold of the box at one side and pushed it a little away
> from the bars, so that he could have easily reached the
> prize. But he walked off without paying any attention
> to it. The test was broken off here, as Sultan appeared
> from its inception, indifferent and indisposed to take
> trouble. A little later, after the box had been replaced
> at the bars, the young animals were all let into the
> room. Only Rana shook the box a little, but did not
> move it away, and presently Sultan, obviously excited
> by the competition, " took a hand ", removed the
> obstacle, and pulled in the objective with a stick.

Here is how Chica behaved in the same kind of
situation :

> Finally, just as we were about to break off the test,
> thinking our waiting futile, Chica suddenly struck the
> right solution, she propped her back against the bars of
> the cage, thrust sideways at it with all four limbs and,
> thrusting it back, grasped the fruit. She had to exert
> her full strength as Tercera had seated herself on the
> top of the box, and remained enthroned with impassive
> countenance throughout the proceedings."

What will the ape do if the food is very high up,
too high to be reached by jumping ? Can the animal
move a box across the cage, stand on it and reach his
objective ? Having achieved this, can he learn, if

the food is placed higher still, to put boxes one on top of the other, mount them and gain the food? The answer is Yes; and here are descriptions of Sultan, Grande and Chica at work:

> Sultan has fasted all forenoon and, therefore, goes at his task with great zeal. He lays the heavy box flat underneath the objective, puts the second one upright upon it, and standing on the top, tries to seize the objective. As he does not reach it, he looks down and round about, and his glance is caught by the third box, which may have seemed useless to him at first, because of its smallness. He climbs down very carefully, seizes the box, climbs up with it and completes the construction.
>
> Grande would not allow herself to be diverted by any number of mishaps, the collapse of the erection, or any other difficulties partly created involuntarily by herself, and soon was able to put three boxes on top of each other, like Sultan. She even managed once a beautiful construction of four boxes. Chica also built towers composed of three boxes without too many mishaps, but has not become so expert as Grande, because, impatient and quick by nature, she prefers dangerous jumps from the floor or from some low structure, to the slow process of building.

Before we consider what such achievements mean, both for the ape, and for our discussion of learning in general, let us look at a few of the things which proved too difficult for the apes. Some of them were not able, for example, to move a box and use it to build with, if at the time they wanted it a companion was seated on it. Furthermore, even though they could put boxes one on top of the other, leap on them and get the food safely, they never built really stable structures despite their frequent practice at such an operation. Then, unwinding a rope, neatly coiled round the branch of a tree, in order to swing on it towards the fruit, caused great difficulty ; the apes pulled at these coils in a way that indicated that their simple winding round the branch was not apparent to them. A similar almost insurmountable difficulty arose when it was necessary, in order to use a stick, to lift it first off a nail or rod to which it was attached by means of an iron ring.

What is the essential difference between these situations in which the ape can and cannot achieve a solution ? If we put ourselves in his position it seems perhaps equally easy for us to see that a rope can be unwound when it is simply coiled round a branch, as it does, say, to use a stick in order to reach the food just outside our reach : in both cases we ' see ' what should be done. But supposing the rope appeared to us, not as simply looped round the branch, but tied in such a tangle of knots that we could not trace it through and through, then we should find that problem more difficult even though we would know that knots can eventually be un- ravelled. Or supposing we had never met separately either the ring or the nail, then such a structure might appear as an entity which we might not think of attempting to disconnect. All this means that an important part of achieving anything is the ability to break up the mass of objects which surround us into real units. In some cases the ape is able to do this ; for example, he is able to break up the situation in which the box is against the bars of the cage, and move it successfully so that the fruit is accessible, but the same ape who has done this is unable to use a box to build with, when a companion is seated on it. Apparently the ' seat function ' which the box has at that time is so firmly established that no other function can be ascribed to it.

Consider another of the ape's failures ; they never made a really stable structure of boxes despite the number of times they made their piles. Why ? Because stacking boxes in a stable fashion was never something that the ape aimed at, wanted, or ' saw ' as a problem to be solved. The unstable pile served the purpose and helped him to reach the food. This shows us that despite frequent practice and repetition an action *need* not be learned if it is never envisaged as a problem and never aimed at. In order that an intelligent action may arise then, the world, as the ape sees it, must be broken up into parts, must be broken so that tools are discovered and used and obstructions removed ; furthermore, something must be aimed at, some end must seem desirable.

What else can the ape's achievements and failures teach us ? There is the successful use of the stick to bridge the gap between the arm and the fruit ; this is in a sense the converse of the breaking up of the total situation ; things that are not at the moment joined together can be made so, because parts of the world, which normally for the ape have quite other functions, can be made to yield their services. At first it is only those things which are obviously in a position, ready to be used. At first, the stick had to be in the cage and in full view of the ape as he looks at the fruit, but after this had been achieved, advances were possible within this new behaviour itself, such that two disconnected sticks would be joined to do the work.

Learning, we said, has several aspects : one of these, achieving an intelligent action for the first time, we have now considered, but there are also actions which have no clear-cut first time, which are somehow bound up with the physical development of the organism and which emerge slowly and at their own time, yet require a long period in which they are being learned. Such activities are, for example, creeping, grasping objects, walking, and the colossal achievement of language, all part of the normal development of the human being. So let us now look into a laboratory, or experimental nursery, and watch human twins, Johnny and Jimmy, performing for us.

The question in the mind of the investigator who undertook this work was whether training can hasten the development of these activities which appear in the individual life history of all human beings at approximately the same time, and similarly, whether training can facilitate the development of more specialized activities which do not necessarily become

part of each individual's equipment, and do not manifest themselves spontaneously and uniformly. Before
we discuss these experiments, however, we must say
a word about the technique involved here, for they
are experiments not only pertinent to our question
concerning learning and development, but also illus-
trative of an interesting method.

The psychologist frequently wishes to make comparisons between individuals, or groups of individuals ;
in such comparisons his aim is to have the individuals
as nearly alike as possible, except for the one factor,
the importance or influence of which he wishes to
determine. Experiments often consist in giving the
same task to the ' critical ' and ' control ' groups in
the expectation that the factor or quality possessed by
the critical group alone may show up in the performance of this group. In the realm of child psychology, nature has provided the experimentalist with
a perfect ' control ' : for identical twins, of course,
furnish two individual subjects as nearly alike as it
is possible for them to be. If we train one twin (T),
and leave the other twin on any specific activity as
a control (C), then what appears in the behaviour of
T in a given instance where training has been employed, over and above what appears in the behaviour
of C, may safely be ascribed to the influence of the
particular training.

But we are going too fast, for there are interesting
questions involved even in ascertaining how complete
is the similarity between the two individuals. Granted

that they look 'identical', and granted that finer methods of observation show even the markings on their fingers and their bodily measurements to be the same, the psychologist can still ask is their behaviour, or rather, are certain behaviour patterns, identical too ? Applied science in the guise of films has made the answer to this question possible, and provides the experimenter with a fascinating as well as an instructive pursuit.

By filming twins in identical situations at the same hours over long periods of time, it is possible to get an accurate record of what each does and to compare actions point for point, movement for movement, in an amazingly exact manner. Such records have shown a great similarity in what each twin does in a given situation. For example, one pair of twins who were studied in detail were presented with a small pellet when they were consecutively 28, 38, 40 and 42 weeks old. They were both oblivious of the pellet at 28 weeks, but at 38 weeks made a few simple hand movements towards it which were described as almost 'uncanny' in their similarity. At 40 weeks old more complicated hand movements were made in each case almost identical. The analysed records showed 513 identical movements out of a total of 612.

In making a comparison between twins, therefore, the psychologist is equipped to make a very detailed study. Remembering this, let us now watch Johnny and Jimmy. Johnny, being the less active baby at birth is chosen for the twin who is to be trained ; this is obviously a safeguard against any uncontrolled advantage going to the twin who is to play the critical rôle. Johnny therefore is 'stimulated' at two-hour intervals during his working day in the laboratory in those activities which are within his scope at the time. Jimmy, on the other hand, is kept from such stimulation. When Johnny first shows evidence of a desire to crawl, for example, he is placed in a jacket on which are some kind of rollers, and suspended in such a way that, his weight being removed from his own arms and legs, his progress would be considerably easier. Again, when later he shows a desire to achieve an upright posture, or to make movements towards walking, he is assisted and trained in this procedure. Meanwhile Jimmy is left to his own devices, and the question arises, has this consistent training actually speeded up Johnny's performance and improved it ? The answer in the case of the two foregoing examples, together with such activities as assuming a sitting posture, grasping, reaching for an object, and the like, is No ; untrained Jimmy was at no disadvantage, these activities developed freely and at the same time as they did in the 'exercised' Johnny. When Jimmy was tested after a period of no training he was found to be as advanced as his trained twin.

There are other points of interest here in addition to this result : we find the experimenter reaching the same conclusion as was found in certain phases of the ape's learning, namely, " Mere exercise will not neces-

sarily result in an improvement." In the case of the
apes it was necessary that something be aimed at before
learning could progress ; in this case it is necessary
for the organism to be ' ready ' for that particular
pattern of behaviour to find expression. " Exercise ",
this experimenter concludes, " may influence the grace
with which the child steps but it will not advance
the day a child begins to walk alone and will not alter
the general method of progression." This general
method of progression is another interesting point, for
here we have an indication of the pattern of development common to many activities, an indication of the
stages whereby " practice makes perfect ". No pattern
of behaviour such as walking, crawling or sitting
appears fully developed at one given time. Nor are
there any sharp lines of demarcation as it progresses
through consecutive stages. There are, however,
periods of rapid development and improvement,
spurts, which are followed by periods of inactivity.
Sometimes several components in the general pattern
will be markedly exaggerated, one particular action
will be pronounced at the expense of others. Such
exaggerated features will eventually curtail each other
so that finally smooth and easy performance will result
and the child will no longer be learning to walk, but
will walk as a matter of course.

We may now turn to a comparison of a different
type of behaviour in Johnny and Jimmy. Whereas
the former performances belong to all human development, Johnny is now confronted with and trained in,

situations which he need not ever develop the ability to handle or react to. During this training period, Jimmy is as usual left without these activities, and is later tested to see how he fares in a similar situation.

From the various situations in which Johnny was placed we have selected several to serve as examples, in that they have the added interest of being somewhat similar to those with which the apes were presented. For instance, food is placed on the top of a high stool, too high for Johnny to reach ; but in the room and available for use are several other light stools of different sizes, which may be easily pushed into positions so as to form stepping-stones to the higher stool on which the food is placed. How does Johnny tackle such a problem during his days of free access to the stools ? The first stage seems to be one of merely looking at the inaccessible food. This is followed by a stage in which a vague and easily disturbed ' connection ' is made between some stools and the high stool itself. This connection is easily broken, for after making a move to push a stool in the direction of the food, Johnny may somehow lose the ' idea ' and push the stool off somewhere else. This is reminiscent of the behaviour of some of the chimpanzees, who you will remember would pick up a stick, as if to use it to advantage, and then let it drop again.

The next step involves bringing the lower stool near the high one, and, if he can mount this one and reach the food the problem is probably solved. But the one stool that he brings may be too low ; consequently he must now achieve the accumulation of more than one stool, placed in a step-ladder series. In doing this the exaggerated phase which we spoke of may be apparent ; for instance, the child will bring many stools, some quite unnecessary for the solution, and place them all alongside. Finally he will begin to discriminate and to bring only those stools necessary for stepping up from the ground to the food.

Johnny began his training, or the period in which he was free to exercise himself with regard to this problem, when he was under two years, 539 days old to be exact. It took him until he was 582 days to master this situation so that he would select the necessary two stools in order to mount to the highest stool. The problem was then varied so that the object hung from the ceiling ; this introduced new difficulties, and it was not until he was 714 days old, or fully two years that he had mastered this. Even so he still brought more stools than were absolutely necessary in order to reach the food.

Jimmy, without training, was 665 days old when he was first allowed to play in this same setting. But at this age, several months after Johnny had conquered his first problem, Jimmy was unable to utilize the stools for climbing. He only pushed the stools around, but made no attempt to arrange them or climb on them. As one would expect, therefore, daily exercise in such an activity develops it rapidly, Johnny's performance as a result of his training being unique among children under two years old.

Another problem situation is interesting, as it again closely approximates that given to the apes, namely, the piling of boxes one on top of the other in order to reach the food hung from the ceiling. Johnny at 595 days old, is able, after a week, to place one box on top of another. At 613 days old he is able to climb on the small box and then on the larger. At 725 days he could select and stack boxes with regard to their size and with respect to the height of the suspended food.

We have drawn attention to the similarity of such a situation to the building which was demanded from the apes, but there is also one very important difference involved here ; the apes were strong and adept in handling boxes before they embarked on their specific problem. Johnny in the situation here described is learning both to handle stools and boxes, climb on them, and at the same time solve his problem with regard to the food.

Jimmy, called in unpractised when Johnny has achieved this, was unable, despite his advanced age and increased bodily development at the time of first tackling the problem, to get beyond pushing the boxes around. Johnny and Jimmy therefore, individuals who are virtually identical as far as development, potentialities and abilities are concerned, have answered a question for the psychologist. They have shown that whereas training will rapidly advance those performances which every individual may or may not acquire for himself, yet exercise and assistance do not materially advance the behaviour which belongs to the infant by virtue of its being human. This, you may say, is exactly what you would have expected : but there is a good deal of difference between popular belief and accurately controlled knowledge ; moreover, if psychology had proved the opposite, the educator in the home would have had a hard time of it.

We must now turn to the third aspect of learning which we have chosen to discuss, that most nearly akin to what in ordinary usage we mean when we speak of learning, that is, the conscious endeavour to master a specific task.

The question now arises what kind of a task ? I may wish to ' learn to type ', to ' learn to skate ', to ' learn a foreign vocabulary ', to ' learn mathematics ' : the same word but a different learning process in each case.

If I wish to learn to skate, my problem is essentially one of acquiring certain bodily movements and balance. These can only be learned by my discovering how they ' feel ', for I may know a skating text-book by heart and still fall down every time I try to cut a figure 8.

In learning to type I must also acquire bodily movements but of a rather limited kind ; moreover, in addition, I must learn to co-ordinate them with mental processes. I shall gradually advance in this case from a restricted stage of slowness and uncertainty, to the point where I automatically press the correct keys after having read a whole phrase.

In learning a foreign vocabulary by heart I may do so as a pure routine performance, without understanding the words I learn, or as part of a comprehension of language in general and this language in particular. My ' pure routine ' learning, would involve psychologically, quite a different performance from that which is involved when I learn with understanding.

Finally, I may wish to learn mathematics ; here bodily movement and pure rote learning will be at a minimum, for my progress will depend on my insight and understanding of an ever-widening system of knowledge.

Intricately bound up with all such problems is a phase of learning which we have so far not even mentioned, and which deserves a chapter to itself, namely, our ability to remember what we have learned. In a sense it is artificial to speak of learning in any phase apart from memory, but again, for convenience, we segregate those problems of learning on which emphasis is placed on the initial acquiring period, from those in which the interest centres on remembrance of what has been learned.

The things which the psychologist looks for differ in each of the learning situations just outlined. For instance, in the acquiring of skill in typing he may concentrate on watching how this habit develops. For, after all, typing is nothing more than a good and useful habit, a personal automatic form of behaviour. Bad habits we frequently deplore, but our good habits seldom receive recognition as such. The habit of typing, in its process of being formed, will be studied from the moment when the subject first begins his somewhat vague handling of the keys until he has attained speed and accuracy. One way of keeping track of his progress will be in terms of his errors during a certain time, and the speed which he is acquiring. Naturally one will expect the first to decrease, the second to increase, but accurate records prove that almost all performances pass through periods of rapid progress followed by periods in which apparently no progress is made, or a lower level of achievement may even be returned to. Learning to type will also lend itself to the determination of what conditions give the best results, for instance, how the practice periods should be spaced, how long they should be, and the like. Such questions may have a wider theoretical significance in addition to their practical applications : What does it mean with reference to the learning process that a particular distribution of practice periods is the most advantageous ?

In learning by heart, an activity which has such an obvious counterpart in memory, determining the conditions under which most can be learned, and under which most can be remembered, has concerned the psychologist ; these we will return to in our chapter on memory and need not elaborate here.

Experimental work on understanding and insight, such as might be illustrated in the learning of mathematics, has not been developed to any great extent by the psychologist ; however, strange as it may seem at first sight, essentially the same questions are pertinent here as were asked from the experiments with the apes. What features in the situation allow relevant connections to be seen ; what features block this insight ? It may seem a far cry from understanding a mathematical relationship in a flash, to seeing the connection between a stick and the banana, but psychologically they are perhaps more akin than mathematical insight is to pure rote learning !

Page 95.   Cf. E. L. Thorndike, *Animal Intelligence*
            (New York, 1911).
,,   95 ff. These pages are based on W. Köhler's *The
            Mentality of Apes* (London and New York,
            1925), from which the quotations are taken.
,,   103 ff. Cf. M. B. McGraw, *Growth ; A Study of Johnny
            and Jimmy* (New York, 1935).
,,   104.   Cf. A. Gesell's article in the *Handbook of
            Child Psychology*. Ed. by C. Murchinson
            (Worcester, Mass., 1931), and Gesell and
            Thompson, *Genetic Psychology Monographs*,
            No. 6.
,,   106 f. Cf. M. B. McGraw, *loc. cit.*

CHAPTER VI

HOW WE LEARN AND REMEMBER

PERHAPS no aspect of mental life has so continuously intrigued the layman as his ' memory ' : for on those occasions when our memory fails us, we are brought face to face with an apparent lack of co-operation in our own organism which may be annoying and embarrassing.

For centuries people have speculated as to what happens when facts are remembered and available for use, or forgotten beyond recall. That memory was some kind of wax tablet on which impressions were made, and were subject to obliteration by the addition of further impressions, was an idea proposed by the philosopher Locke in the seventeenth century ; even earlier we find Hamlet saying, " Yea from the table of my memory I'll wipe away all trivial fond record," a statement which Shakespeare may well have meant to be taken literally.

The difficulty facing the psychologist is that, as usual, he is forced to adopt indirect methods with regard to his problem : he cannot look into someone's head and watch what happens in the brain when the

116

multiplication table or a new language is learned,
keeping track of that happening in the interval and
being present to watch what it does when the time
arrives for the answer to 8 times 12 to be given! He
does not even know directly whether any actual
change in the brain occurs; he can only speculate
on the basis of the results of carefully planned experiments, which in a roundabout way can tell him
whether it can be said that something in the nature
of a wax tablet exists or whether perhaps some sort of
' process ' occurs in the brain when we ' remember '.
He can, in fact, only arrange and change the conditions under which people learn, and those under which
they show that they remember what they have learned.

Let us run through some of these conditions which
are amenable to such experimental variation. The
experimenter can control what the subject is made to
learn, prose, poetry, numbers, foreign words, signs and
so on. He can control the amount that the subject
is given, and how it is presented, that is, in its entirety
or in parts. He can control the time that the subject
spends in studying the material on each occasion, and
the number of these occasions, the interval between
them, and what is done in these intervals. He can
control the age of his subjects, their physical conditions
and their previous experience with the material to be
learned, that is, whether it is familiar or entirely new
to them. In a similar way he can control the occasions
on which the subject is asked to recall what he has
learned, the duration of each attempt, the interval

between attempts, the condition of the subject at the time of recalling.

In addition, he can control the manner in which the recall is made : he may simply say ' tell me all you remember ', and see what that brings forth, or he may give the subject certain key-words and then ask him to tell what these words lead him to recall. Finally, the experimenter may show the subject certain parts of what he has learned, together with similar material which he has actually not seen, and ask for the identification or recognition of the items or parts already seen.

In a consideration of such factors the layman's interest is probably somewhat practical ; he has an eye to seeing how he can help himself to remember his own particular tasks, but the psychologist is interested as much in the exhibition of bad memory and failure as he is in accurate recall, for what he is aiming at is to discover what kind of phenomenon memory is.

Let us begin with a consideration of the effect on memory of the different kinds of material memorized, or, why some things are more easily remembered than others. It is a commonplace that poetry is easier to learn and remember than prose, and prose of our own tongue infinitely easier than prose of a foreign language. Similarly prose that is meaningful will be learned far more easily than a mere jumble of words or a mere disconnected list of figures. But the question is why ?

The answer that you will give spontaneously will serve as an introduction : " Poetry," you will say,

" has rhythm, it swings along ; further it has rhyme, and rhyme gives one clues, therefore it is easier to remember. And as to sensible prose as compared to nonsense, that goes without saying, for I am familiar with the one while the other is quite new to me. In a sense I have learned any piece of meaningful prose beforehand, because I have already come across words and even sentences in it, and that is why I remember it better."

Exactly ! These are very useful observations, but let us see what they mean to the psychologist. He would agree with you that because you are familiar with the words, because they are meaningful and already part of your experience, in some way, they are more easily remembered. But this fact that they are already part of your experience has to some extent increased his difficulties, for as you will remember, he is aiming at controlling his situations in the strictest sense. How then can he start from scratch, so to speak, how can he study memory *per se* if the subject has already partially memorized any piece of prose or poetry with which he is presented ?

This difficulty led one of the early psychologists, Ebbinghaus by name, to plan experiments in memory in which he used only ' nonsense ' material, for, he argued, I must have brand new, unfamiliar, unrelated material before I can study accurately how it is best learned, best remembered and by what stages or laws it is forgotten. He then evolved what are known as the *nonsense syllables*. These syllables he arranged in

pairs and learned in lists of varying length. For
example :

        lun . . . mus
        pos . . . fip
        del . . . nux
        nef . . . bam

and so on. With these new items for his material
Ebbinghaus could ask questions about the conditions
that facilitated or hindered recall, feeling that he had
eliminated factors of previously established memories
which might falsify his results.

He tested his own memory for these syllables by
repeating the entire list ; subsequent investigators
employed the additional method of being presented
with the first of any pair, and then attempting to recall
the syllable which had gone with it.

Certain conditions, Ebbinghaus and his followers
found, facilitated their learning and their ability to
recall. For example, they learned faster when the
syllables were recited in a marked iambic rhythm,
that is with regular emphasis on the second syllable,
than they were when there was no such accent given.
They found that spacing the learning periods reduced
the number of repetitions needed in order to be word
perfect on the whole list. Some syllables proved to
be better remembered than others, namely those at the
beginning and end of the list ; it was possible also to
determine the length of the list which gave the greatest
economy of time spent in learning and accuracy of
recall. Certain conditions proved detrimental to

accurate recall : if the syllable *mus*, which in the list in question is to be learned as the partner of *lun*, had on a previous occasion been associated and learned together with another syllable, let us say *pob*, then it required more repetitions in the learning period before it could be correctly reproduced with *lun*. Or again, if the learning periods were interspersed with other occupations, some of these occupations in and of themselves affected the subsequent ability to recall ; some ways of spending the intervening period damaged what had been learned more than others. Ebbinghaus also found that he could make a general statement about the rate of forgetting, namely, that during the first hours relatively much is forgotten, followed by a more gradual loss of the remaining material.

We have, then, reliable information concerning memory under controlled conditions, but the fact still remains that this carefully controlled nonsense material is much harder to learn than the ordinary material of everyday life, and the question arises as to whether what has been gained in accuracy has not been lost by the introduction of unnatural and artificial conditions.

What constitutes the peculiar difficulty of these nonsense syllables ? In order to answer this we must consider the theoretical side of the question ; or, put in another way, must ask what light did these experiments throw on the assumption that memory was in the nature of a wax tablet ? As a matter of fact, they somewhat reinforced it, for they seemed to require that, in order that the isolated item *mus* be remembered as following on *lun*, they must in some way be joined together, and what more natural than to think of this ' joining ' in and of itself as another impression on the wax, a bond that would be strengthened, deepened, or further impressed every time *lun* and *mus* were repeated together ?   On this assumption meaningful material, having bonds already joining its associated items, would be more easily recalled, while nonsense syllables, with no such established linkage, would require a great many repetitions to provide an adequately strong bond between them.

At this point we have to become critical : are we satisfied with this type of explanation, and, more important, do the facts really support it ?   Theoretically it will be seen to be out of harmony with our general approach.   If, for good reasons, we have elsewhere rejected all mechanical explanations as the basic concepts underlying behaviour, then we must be wary of this mechanical explanation, this suggestion that ' impressions made on wax ' is the best interpretation of that which underlies, and is the counterpart of, such a vital phenomenon as memory.   But more important than this is the question of whether the facts support the view that the essence of good memory lies in the strength of the bonds which are established between separate items, and that the difficulty inherent in the nonsense syllables lies in the fact that the bonds have to be established then and there.

From certain experiments, however, it would seem as if this were not really the case : the difficulty in

learning and recalling a list of nonsense syllables seems
rather to lie in the homogeneity of such a list, its lack
of landmarks, its uniformity, rather than in the new
connections which have to be formed. Our evidence
for this is the fact that when some of these same nonsense syllables, which in and of themselves have proved
difficult to remember, are interspersed in lists composed
in the main of other uniform items (say pairs of numbers), then these syllables rather than the more familiar
but more uniform items, are better remembered.

So we come back to a very fundamental point : it
is the total situation and not only isolated parts of it
which must tell us the story. In other words, it
matters what something is ' learned with ', it matters
what the wider setting to any psychological event is.
In this case the ' residue ' from the different parts of
what has been learned may be said to affect and be
affected by the ' residue ' from other parts. Even in
Ebbinghaus's original experiments we had an illustration of just this. The characteristics of the activity
which followed the learning of the list of nonsense
syllables actually affected the subsequent remembrance
of them, and additional experiments since then have
shown that the more similar the intervening activity
becomes to the original learning, the less accurate and
full is the recall of the original, a point which we shall
have to elaborate later on.

However, since this is the case, it is hard to substantiate the hypothesis that this ' residue ' is something equivalent to an isolated scratch on wax, for

an isolated scratch cannot affect other scratches. We should then be justified in saying that a better hypothesis might be the assumption that, whatever its nature, this residue is at least subject to change and distortion, reinforcement and consolidation, by the influence of other processes which may be occurring, or even other residua left from such processes.

Such an idea is by no means new to us. In Chapter I we saw how this kind of interaction occurred in natural processes, and as we have passed in review the various fields of psychological investigation we have seen the influence of one part of experience on another, this indication that mental life is not built out of discrete bricks. The work with the nonsense syllables, how-ever, was of great importance to psychology at the time at which it was done, calling attention as it did to the possibility of treating experimentally even the ' higher mental processes ' themselves.

In continuing our discussion of memory we may now turn to investigations which have recognized the arti-ficial aspects of the nonsense material, and have realized the dangers of assuming that robbing the material to be learnt of all meaning, necessarily implies the reduction of the psychological response to its simplest and purest form. In these investigations conditions more akin to those of our natural environ-ment have been employed, and yet results of theoretical significance have been obtained

We called attention elsewhere to the indirect way in which the psychologist is forced to work : it would be simple indeed if, at intervals over a period of a year let us say, he could lift the lid off the brain and observe what was happening to that which remained, the residue, of a given experience. The indirect way in which he is forced to get an answer to such a question is to ask the subject to reproduce what he remembers, at given intervals, over a period of weeks or months. If what is remembered changes during these successive reproductions, showing a tendency to become different from what it was originally along certain lines, then we may at least make suggestions as to what may be happening in the brain to parallel such changes.

Let us give a concrete example : the Figs. 10 and 11

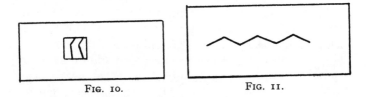

FIG. 10.   FIG. 11.

were shown to the subject. After a period of time what the subject reproduced as having seen originally, were Figs. 12 and 13.

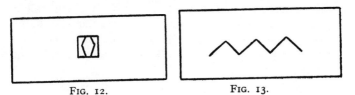

FIG. 12.   FIG. 13.

What can we assume about the nature of the 'residue' of this original experience? First, it is quite clear that it has not simply faded out or been obliterated : on the other hand, it is not the same as the original. Furthermore, each drawing differs from the original in a different way. Fig. 12 shows what we might call a simplification, it has become more regular and symmetrical ; Fig. 13, on the other hand, has become 'sharper', there is an exaggeration of or over-emphasis of certain aspects at the expense of others. On our hypothesis, then, it seems reasonable to suppose that whatever happenings in the brain have given rise to such changed reproductions were, in the course of time, themselves changed along these lines.

Let us take another example ; in this case instead of one and the same subject repeatedly reproducing what he has seen, a number of subjects each see as the 'original material' the reproduction made by another subject. For instance, subject A will, after an interval of time, reproduce a drawing that he has been shown, subject B will be shown A's reproduction and subsequently be asked to reproduce that. What will be the reproduction that is given by the last of, say, 20 subjects, how will it differ from the original picture, and will those same tendencies of simplification and exaggeration, manifested by one subject when he alone repeats the drawings over a period of time, show up in this other procedure in which a series of different subjects take part ?

Here is a very striking example : Fig. 14 a is the

original drawing shown to the first subject : his reproduction of it (Fig. 14 b) is easily recognizable and is
what might well be expected.   But without the intervening 18 drawings the next figure (14 c), reproduced
by subject 19 as what he remembers having been
shown, is rather a surprise !

To show how this cat ever came about we must

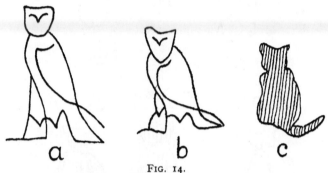

a   b   c

FIG. 14.
From Bartlett : " Remembering."

reproduce the drawings of subjects number 4, 6, 8, 9,
10, and 14.

Are the same changes of ' simplification ' and
' elaboration ' visible in this series also ?   It seems so ;
Fig. 15 e is simpler than Fig. 15 d ; that is, the reproduction of subject 6 is simpler than that of subject 4.
On the other hand, there is an elaboration of certain
details evidenced in the drawing of subject 10 over
that of subject 9 with which he was presented originally ; while by the fourteenth reproduction (Fig. 15 i)

the very simple figure has been reached which does not vary for the last four subjects.

A further study of what happens when the subjects

Fig. 15.
From Bartlett : " Remembering."

are asked to give these repeated reproductions shows that, if the original drawings are somewhat ambiguous, these tendencies to simplification and elaboration result in the reproductions approximating well-known and familiar objects ; moreover, such ambiguous figures will almost certainly be named by the subject, with the result that the successive reproductions will undergo a closer and closer approximation to the thing to which the original drawing was likened.

When the material to be reproduced is prose and not a drawing, other interesting facts come to light. Most striking are the consistent omissions of unfamiliar names or elements, and of those aspects of the story which do not find obvious support in the accepted cultural background of the subject. Equally important is the rationalization and the creating of a more ' coherent, concise and undecorated tale ' by the addition of links in the argument which make for a greater unity and which sharpen the point of the story as a whole.

From such accounts it can be seen that memory is very far from being the passive registration of external happenings with an unerring and inevitable reproduction of them ; rather, it gives evidence of being a constructive activity of the organism and one which results from the arousal of dynamic processes.

Let us go back for a moment to that point in our experience when we perceive that which we may subsequently be asked to remember, to the moment when the ' impression is made '. When we discussed earlier some problems of visual experiences we emphasized that perceiving is likewise not a passive reception from the outside world, the organism being active in this process also. Here is a nice illustration : blotches of the following kind were shown to a number of observers :

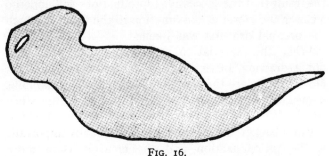

FIG. 16.
From Bartlett : " Remembering."

This particular figure was seen by different observers as a seal, snail, slug, mermaid, fish, whale, dragon without eyes, Roman lamp, man lying in a sack, and a tadpole : needless to say, if the original seeing of this object lends itself to such variation, the recall of this same item by the different observers will also vary. So we find that, in addition to the general tendencies of simplification and elaboration, individual interest, attitudes and the cultural background from which the subject comes, will enter into both perception and the recall of a given object.

Let us now turn to experiments of a slightly different kind, but which again bear out our general assumption : the experimenter in this case gave her subjects about a score of small tasks to do, such as modelling a clay figure, naming poets and cities beginning with the same letter, and so on, allowing them to finish some of these tasks and cutting short the others. When she tested her subjects later to see how many of these tasks they remembered having done, she found that almost twice as many of the unfinished as the finished were recalled and enumerated. The same result was found when jokes, some finished and some left ' hanging in the balance ', were told to the subject who had subsequently to say which one he remembered.

The experiments on the unfinished tasks are worth our further attention in that they show the care which must be exercised before a conclusion is reached, and the kind of questions the experimenter must ask himself.   Here is a result : the unfinished tasks are better remembered than the finished ones, but the question is *why ?*

It might well be that these specific tasks were, for some reason, easier to remember than the others, that the critical factor only *seemed* to lie in their unfinished aspect. That is easily checked ; the experimenter must reverse the procedure, the tasks originally finished must be interrupted, those originally left unfinished completed ; this of course will be done with another ' control ' group of subjects. When this was done, however, the answer remained the same : the new unfinished tasks were then better remembered by this group of subjects. Has that settled the question ? Not quite : it might be that the subjects expected to finish these tasks at some later time, and this expectation accounted for their being remembered. How can the experimenter get around this difficulty ? By telling yet another group of subjects that these unfinished tasks would not be resumed at a later date, and again making the comparison. When despite this the results are still in favour of the unfinished tasks, it looks as if their unfinished character was indeed the crucial one.

Their unfinished character, that is, as far as the individual subject is concerned ; that is an important point, to which we shall refer later, for it shows the interconnectedness of the ' self ' with the activities undertaken. What does this mean, and how are we justified in saying it ? Because it is possible for a task, actually completed according to instructions, to appear unfinished to a subject ; and conversely a task unfinished according to the instructions may appear finished to the subject. To take an example : the experimenter may make the task : " Throw three darts at that target and try and hit a bull's-eye." Each of the three shots may nearly hit the mark but not quite. Now when the subject has actually finished the task set him it may well be that he feels " With one more dart I could have done it ", so that as far as he is concerned the task is still incomplete. The converse is exemplified in such a task as, " Translate this passage from the Greek ", when the subject possesses no knowledge of Greek. In this case the subject might well consider the experiment finished as far as he is concerned because of the impossibility of his even attempting to follow the instructions. The point of

all this is that as far as their ' memory-value ' is concerned, it is how the tasks appear to the subject that
is all important. Tasks which were completed tech-
nically but were still felt by the subject to be incomplete, were remembered, as were the unfinished jokes,
better than the completed ones.

We are free now to speculate as to the meaning
of this finding, namely, that tasks left unfinished, left
hanging in the balance, stand a greater chance of being
remembered than the same kind of tasks which are
completed and done with. Let us take a cue from
these phrases of ordinary usage, ' left hanging in the
balance ' or ' left in mid-air ' ; what do they mean ?
Obviously they indicate a state of suspense, they
epitomize tension and strain. Might we not assume,
then, that the unfinished tasks are represented by some
occurrence, some residue in the brain which is also in
a state of tension, which is, in accordance with previously stated principles, seeking to reduce its tension
and re-establish a state of equilibrium ? In other
words, the residue in this state of tension might be
thought of as more active than that which underlies
a completed task where no such tension is involved,
and as a result of this greater activity more likely to
give rise to, or cause, processes of recall or remembrance.

No discussion of learning or memory is complete
without a consideration of that problem known to the
psychologist as the ' transfer of training ', or, how much

does learning and practice in one activity contribute towards and carry over into learning and progress in another ?

Of course we all implicitly assume that some such ' transfer ' occurs ; we should never expect to have to learn every single activity without reference to what has been learned in an allied situation. But, and there's the rub, as psychologists we must ask what constitutes an ' allied situation ' ? You would expect to find, for example, that learning to cut a figure 3 on the ice would be greatly facilitated by having previously learned a figure 8. But would you expect your practice on the ice to carry over to roller skating ? You would certainly say off hand that learning to solve an algebraic problem would aid in solving others of the same type, but would you say that such learning would render geometry easier to grasp ? Of this you may not be so sure.

The task of the psychologist therefore is to try to determine accurately in what phases of behaviour this ' carry-over ' actually occurs, and to discover by virtue of what laws it operates, within the more general framework of what is known about other aspects of learning and memory.

In the light of what we have said in this and the previous chapter let us see what we can say about ' transfer '. It all comes back, of course, to the way the ' residue ' left from a previous activity plays into the new situation. And when we speak of this ' residue ' we are considering, as before, what remains from those processes which must have occurred in the brain during previous activity and experience.

We all know for instance that a poem, the multiplication table, a list of words, or even nonsense syllables, become easier and easier to learn by heart each time they are repeated. Here there is the very obvious contribution made by the ' residue ' left from the previous recital. But we have also noted that there are some cases where certain activities which intervene between the learning and its recall make it more difficult for the subject to remember what he has learned. Here the ' residue ' of the intervening activity introduces difficulties. Cases in which transfer of training occurs, then, must belong here also, for in cases of transfer the ' residue ' of some previous activity is brought into play so as to facilitate (or hinder) the new performance.

" But," you may object, " we are still without the answer as to what constitutes such a situation : it must not be identical with the original one, for then you do not call it transfer, nor must it involve an activity completely and utterly different from the original, for then there would be nothing which could be transferred." The psychologist, I think, will have to admit that he has not as yet succeeded in accurately mapping out this province, but from this you can see where his problems lie.

Let us turn now to some actual experimental work, taking as our subject the white rat. We have previously spoken of the mazes in which the rat is placed and in which he is allowed to run until he has learned the correct pathways to the food without useless excursions into blind alleys. The diagram in Fig. 17 may illustrate more clearly what such a maze is like.

Now, of course, in reference to this problem, mazes may be constructed so as to vary from each other by small deviations only, or may be made on entirely different patterns. In this case we can ask the question, " Will the rat benefit from his experiences in the

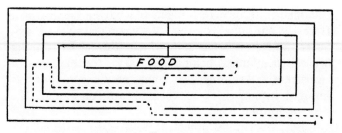

FIG. 17.

first maze which he learns in any or all of the subsequent mazes in which he finds himself, or only in those which are similar in construction to the first, or will this very similarity be confusing? " Such a question allows us to approach the ambiguous ' allied situation ' in a somewhat more concrete way.

The answer to this particular question, as given by one experimenter, was that the rats gained from their previous learning in all the five subsequent mazes in which he tested them, but gained most in that maze which was most similar to the original. However, they also did better in a totally dissimilar maze than the rats who had had no previous training. Presumably, then, what was carried over was a general familiarity with the ' maze situation ', perhaps a lack of initial apprehension.

On the other hand, and showing how complicated this problem is, another experimenter found exactly the opposite result—namely, that previous learning greatly hindered the development of the correct behaviour in a new maze. In this case the maze was a T-shaped one, as shown in Fig. 18.

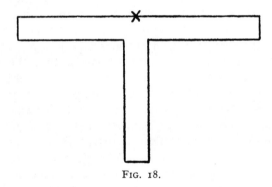

FIG. 18.

The rats had to learn to turn to the right when a light was shown at x and to the left when there was no such light. When this had been mastered the process was reversed, the rats being required to go to the left on seeing a light and to the right for darkness. In this case having learned situation 1 proved a great disadvantage; it required more than twice as many practice periods to establish this second habit as it had taken to establish the first, although, of course, when this ' second ' habit was learned in and of itself it was no more difficult than that used in the original situation.

In contrasting these two maze situations we ought perhaps to add a common-sense warning, for the mazes are admittedly so different in construction, the second being hardly a ' maze ' at all, that no unprejudiced observer would expect the same results to obtain. In the first experiment, by the time the rat has explored and learned maze 1 he may be said to have gained a general familiarity with a maze as such. In the second experiment this factor does not enter in. However, what we wish to contrast is not that the two *mazes* give different results, but rather to point out that the effect of previous training may manifest itself in different ways, either by facilitating the subsequent activities, or by hindering them ; thus we use the terms ' positive ' and ' negative ' transfer respectively. Our theoretical problem, therefore, becomes two-fold : we have not only to discover what type of performance in the individual's past leaves a residue such that it will contribute to a present activity ; but also to discover what direction the influence of this ' residue ' will take ; whether among the possible effects it will block or facilitate the arousal of the processes required for the successful handling of the new situation.

Before we leave this topic of transfer, where, as elsewhere, we have done little more than indicate some of the questions which it falls to the lot of the psychologist to consider, we must mention one aspect which has received much publicity in educational circles during recent years.

That certain subjects, notably the classics, are excellent mind trainers, *per se*, is a doctrine which, even if you were not brought up on it, will have been brought to your attention. But is it a valid assumption that Latin and Greek, in and of themselves, develop the mind so that it is most advantageously equipped to deal with all other subjects? Or is the theory of some modern educators, who emphasize the value of specific training for specific tasks, nearer the truth?

The most systematic investigation made along these lines has shown, I think, that there is relatively little value in this purely formal training, but in so far as any one subject can be considered as superior as general training, it is mathematics rather than classics. In order to reach this conclusion the experimenter followed the progress of several hundred high-school students for a year. These students were divided into several groups, matched in age and intelligence and tested in Selective and Retentional Thinking at the beginning and end of their year's work. The work of one such group, for instance, included three subjects and Latin ; its control group worked on the same subjects but were taught mathematics instead of Latin. Other paired groups were used to test the importance of the inclusion or omission of each of the other subjects. Since, when the second test in thinking was given at the end of the year, those whose training had included mathematics showed the greatest amount of improvement over their previous scores in the first test, the conclusion is reached that mathematics has contributed most to the development of general thinking. Despite this superiority of mathematics, however, the more fundamental conclusion was reached that progress is determined relatively little by the training in any one subject rather than another, for the students who stood highest in the first general test gained more from their year's work, regardless of which subjects they took, than did those who stood lowest in the test.

> The chief reason [writes this experimenter] why good thinkers seem superficially to have been made such by having taken certain school studies, is that good thinkers have taken such studies, becoming better by the inherent tendency of the good to gain more than the poor from any study. When the good thinkers studied Greek and Latin these studies seemed to make good thinking . . . if the abler pupils should all study Physical Education and Dramatic Art these subjects would seem to make good thinkers.

If these carefully controlled experiments have shown that the implicit faith in a purely classical education was not so well founded as was once believed, and if they have emphasized the importance of native intelligence as opposed to the benefit derived from any formal training, we must none the less be on our guard lest such information swing us too far in the opposite direction. As psychologists whose words may carry weight with educators we must beware lest in our anxiety to show the need for specific training for certain specific vocations we unduly discredit a general education. There is real transfer of training : for as the study discussed last has shown, certain essential qualities of mind, clear thinking and honesty, the systematic handling of intellectual difficulties, can be acquired from the study of any subject-matter, with the all-important proviso that the teacher is aware of the necessity to develop such qualities in his pupils.

Page 123 f. The theoretical arguments and experimental
            results given on these pages are derived
            from W. Köhler and H. von Restorff. Cf.
            Koffka's *Principles of Gestalt Psychology*,
            pp. 481 ff.
,, 124   A good presentation of the merits of meaning-
            ful as opposed to nonsense material may be
            found in F. C. Bartlett, *Remembering*.
            Cambridge, 1932. Chap. I.
,, 125.   Cf. Koffka, *loc cit.*, Chap. XI.
,, 127 ff. The material, including the illustrations, for
            this discussion is taken from Bartlett, *loc
            cit.*
,, 130 ff. B. Zeigarnik's ingenious experiments on com-
            pleted and uncompleted tasks are given in
            W. D. Ellis' *Source Book of Gestalt Psychology*
            (London and New York, 1937). The ex-
            periments on jokes were carried out by the
            author of this book. Cf. " Organization in
            Higher Mental Processes ", *Psychologische
            Forschung*, Vol. 17, 1932.
,, 133 ff. For a readable discussion concerning the
            transfer problem see H. E. Garrett, *Great
            Experiments in Psychology* (New York
            and London). For a fuller discussion see W.
            S. Hunter's article, " Experimental Studies
            of Learning ", in *Foundations of Experi-
            mental Psychology* (Worcester, 1929).

CHAPTER VII

THE EMOTIONAL SIDE OF LIFE

WE may begin our chapter on Emotions with one of
the experimental psychologist's contributions to the
world of practical affairs, with a description of an
experiment known as the ' association test ', which
may at first sight appear to belong with the experiments on memory. We mentioned in the last chapter,
as one means of testing the remembrance of nonsense
syllables, the method in which the first pair of such
syllables is presented and the subject asked to recall
its partner. But it is also a recognized psychological
procedure to give a list of words, and ask for ' free
associations ' or ' the first word that comes into your
head '. Supposing I ask you for the first thing that
comes to your mind when I say the word " fire ". If
yesterday you had witnessed the burning of a large
hotel, you might well reply with ' hotel ' ; whereas if
it were a normal winter's day you would more readily
reply with ' log ', ' coal ' or the like.

The use to which this procedure has been put (over
and above that of the psycho-analyst who uses it to
discover your emotional complexes !) is that of detect-

ing the guilt of a suspected person. Suppose for the sake of argument that four people are known to have been in a house at the time when a small red purse containing money and a diamond ring had been stolen, then the guilty one of the four is more likely to say ' red ' on being suddenly asked to reply to ' purse ', and to say ' diamond ' when being asked to reply to ' ring ', than is someone who has not seen the purse, does not know it is red, or that there was a diamond ring in it.

" But," you will interrupt at this point, " surely no one is going to be caught like *that*. If I'd stolen it, ' diamond ' is the last thing I would say ; why, I'd even have a word all ready to answer with, which had absolutely no connection with diamond ring, say, ' table ' : that's innocuous enough." Yes, very possibly the culprit thinks as you do, and for this very reason gives himself away. A word that has ' absolutely no connection ' with the stimulus word is in itself suspicious, but even more important is the speed with which this answer is given. If he has a word all ready to be given that answer is going to pop out very quickly ; if he does not have the answer ready, then looking for an obviously innocuous word is going to take time, and the time that he takes to make his responses is being accurately measured in fractions of a second.

Naturally the conclusion that some one person is guilty does not rest on one answer alone. A series of words is given, some having a direct bearing on the theft, the critical words, and some, the uncritical, having been selected at random. Now on analysing the results it will generally be found that not only will there be something significant in the answers themselves, but that in the case of the guilty person the average ' reaction time ' to the critical words as a group will vary considerably from that to the non-critical words. Incidentally, with an imaginary ' crime ', and a stop-watch, this procedure makes an amusing parlour game !

" But if, as a psychologist," I can hear you commenting, " you are hoping to understand anything about the real experiences of those individuals who are submitting to that association test, then surely it is what they feel, what their emotions are during their responses to the critical and uncritical words, that is of equal importance. Is there no technique whereby you can measure their emotions accurately, for at least emotions manifest themselves in bodily activity ? "

How glad the psychologist would be if he could answer you that there was some method whereby the feelings of a subject could be accurately detected and discriminated ; but this he cannot say at the present time. By your comment, however, you have bridged a gap just as it should be bridged, and justified our inclusion of this experiment at this stage, for despite the fact that in our attempts at written analysis we are forced to divide up experiences and behaviour into parts, considering certain problems under certain headings, in actuality there are no such lines of de-

marcation ; memory, learning and emotional behaviour
are not in watertight compartments.

But to return to our ' culprit ' : even though there
is no one unfailing method by which the psychologist
can detect his emotional experience, there are ways
of measuring certain bodily changes which may occur
during emotion and which can give us some indirect
evidence of what the concomitant experiences are.

That bodily changes are almost always part and
parcel of an emotional experience goes without saying.
How do we know that the dog is angry ? Because
his hair bristles, he barks, growls, his eyes flash and
he runs towards the cat he wishes to attack. When
we are waiting for news concerning the health of a
friend in hospital, our hands are clammy, there is a
sinking feeling in our stomachs, our throats are dry ;
at that moment we have cause to be afraid.

Very accurate investigations of these bodily changes
have been made by the physiologists, who have demon-
strated, for example, how the composition of the blood
alters during intense rage, have pointed out which
parts of the nervous system come into play, to produce
the cold sweat of fear, the dilated pupils, the increased
heart-beat, the hair standing on end. To discuss these
experiments would take us beyond our allotted province, for strictly speaking the average experimental
psychologist is not trained to do the delicate surgery
that is necessary in order to determine these questions.
However, the experimental psychologist, at the same
time that he conducts his association test, can take a

record of the subject's heart-beat, pulse-rate, blood pressure, breathing rates and resistance to a small electric current, this last being known as the psycho-galvanic response. Such measurements may sound formidable, but, apart from somewhat bulky apparatus, they are quite easy to obtain.

The instrument which measures the pulse-rate is strapped on the wrist : each throb of the pulse moves a sensitive lever, which in turn moves a little pointer so poised as to scratch marks on a band of smoked paper moving across an opening at a uniform speed. On this moving paper another lever marks the time in fractions of a second so that we have a graphic record of the speed of the pulse. The recording of heart-beats and of breathing is done in a similar way, each movement of the heart or lungs is registered on smoked paper moving at a uniform speed on which time is also recorded ; consequently, differences in the movements of the heart or lungs are registered spatially. Faster heart-beats, for example, will result in marks closer together, while deeper breaths will be shown by bigger excursions of the pointer.

The psycho-galvanic response manifests itself by a little beam of light moving over a scale. The subject is made part of the circuit of a very weak electric current. Apparently under certain conditions the human body conducts an electric current more readily than under others. If the body offers less resistance to the current which is passing through it, this fact will be registered by the small beam of light, for the current, besides passing through the body, also passes through a galvanometer to the needle of which a small mirror is attached ; this mirror oscillates with the change in current, its excursions being the greater the stronger the current resulting from the decreased resistance of the subject. Now among the conditions which affect this change in resistance are fatigue and depression, sudden changes in attentiveness, changes in physiological conditions and also, apparently, the onset of certain emotions, so that in the association test a word fraught with particular significance and meaning might well result in a change of the body's resistance, a change completely beyond the subject's power of control.

These bodily measurements have yielded us certain results, among them the fact that changes in breathing rates (or, more accurately, the relation of breathing " in " to breathing " out ") and changes in blood pressure apparently accompany the telling of false-hoods ; that situations which frighten the subject result in irregular heart,.pulse and breathing records. And yet at best they are only sidelights on our problem, for, in the first place, there is no invariable pattern of ' irregularity ' in pulse, heart or breathing rates for the different emotions. We cannot say, for instance, that this record shows that it was anger and not general excitement that was felt. And it is the same thing in the case of the psycho-galvanic response ; there is not a fixed amount of decreased resistance for this emotion, another for that. Intense pleasure or anger may equally well set the little beam of light moving relentlessly up the scale. All we can say here is that intensity of emotion apparently correlates with the extensity of the movement of the beam of light, and that the records of changes due to fatigue can be differentiated from those due to some emotional factor.

There is another disadvantage attached to these methods : when the subject experiences genuine emotion, it is more than likely that he will not be trussed up in these recording arrangements, whereas when he is arrayed in them, they, by their very premeditatedness, detract from the spontaneity of the situation which is to call forth the emotion.

We all know how important facial expression is in regard to emotion, in our everyday life. We can generally tell at a glance whether someone whom we meet is angry or delighted to see us. Very small children will respond to a smile or be repulsed by an angry frown, and even a dog will gaze into his master's face as if to gain a clue from it. Studying facial expressions experimentally has been done by the use of models in which various features are detachable and interchangeable, both full face and profile ; and by judging photographs of different emotions. The results of the experiments with photographs may seem surprising at first sight, for it has been found over and over again that even the most well-known emotions are often not recognized as such. Photographs of different emotions will be considered the same, the same observer will call a photograph one emotion one day and another the next. Suggestions by the experimenter such as ' perhaps this is anger ' have a marked effect even if they are erroneous suggestions. In short, it becomes clear that no emotion has one and only one expression such that it is easily or invariably recognized. It has also become clear that no one feature is all important for any one emotion, although it has appeared that to a certain extent the mouth seems to be the more important part in sulkiness, contempt and superiority, while the eyes seem to be the most significant in anger, fear, anxiety, doubt and grief.

The net result of experiments with photographs have led investigators to realize that one single ' still ' photograph is an artificial tool, leading to artificial results, and they have voiced the need for the obvious remedy of moving pictures which will give not only movements and sequences of movements, but the sudden arrests and changes in movements also. It has further been recognized that the significance of any series of muscular movements is relative to the pattern of movements as a whole. Experiments with the adjustable models have led to the same realization of the need for dynamic rather than static experimental material.

These experiments, then, on the bodily and facial expression of emotions have not yielded what we might have at first expected, they have not yielded, that is, a scientifically accurate indication of what is being experienced ; but the inevitable accompaniment of emotion by *some* bodily change is so marked that it led to a famous theory concerning the nature of the emotions. This theory, proposed by two early psychologists, Lange and James, claimed that emotions actually were nothing more than our direct experience of these happenings taking place in the body. Sadness has a certain ' flavour ' as opposed to fear ; that distinct psychological difference was the result of the experience of the activity of the tear glands, as opposed to the experience of ' that sinking feeling '. Try and think of being afraid, they argued, without any of the bodily feelings that go with it, and what has become of your fear ? You have no emotion left, only a purely intellectual understanding of a frightening situation. It is an interesting idea, and one that is worth while investigating for yourself. What is left of *your* emotion of anger when you have eliminated everything that has a bodily expression, the ' getting hot under the collar ', the rapid heart-beat, the dilated pupils, the flushed face ?

We have introduced this theory here largely because the checking of its assumptions provides an interesting example of experimental problems and methods. Science has no use for our rejecting an hypothesis merely because we simply can't believe it. We must do more than just be convinced that fear is something other than clammy hands, cold sweat, dilated pupils and that sinking feeling in our stomachs ; we have to show why we do not subscribe to such a belief. Strictly speaking, in order to describe at all adequately the bodily activity involved in emotion another book would have to be written ; we must be satisfied, therefore, with showing where the psychologist's problem lies.

If emotion is nothing more than our experience of the working of some parts of our bodies, then it follows that if it were rendered impossible for us to experience these happenings, we should not feel any emotion ; and secondly, if it were possible to introduce these same bodily changes by purely chemical means, then according to this theory emotion should be experienced despite the absence of an emotional situation.

Even in the interests of science the psychologist and physiologist cannot go cutting out parts of people's nervous systems in order to see if the people will still be emotional ! However, experiments with animals give an answer to our first question, and such experiments are confirmed by observations on invalids who through misfortune are of necessity in an experimental condition. That branch of the nervous system whose functioning brings about many of the bodily changes which go hand in hand with intense emotion, may be separated from the main nervous system in experimental animals while these animals may still live quite healthful and peaceful lives. By cutting off this section we have deprived the animal of the mechanism and sensations, among others, whereby normally its heart would have been accelerated, its hair made to stand erect and sugar released into the blood stream. Despite the fact that there are then no sensations of

the kind thought by Lange and James to constitute
the emotion of rage in its entirety, these animals, in
this case cats, manifested the usual ' hissing and growl-
ing, showing of the teeth and lifting of the paw to
strike ' when in the presence of a barking dog. Likewise in other experiments dogs with equivalent parts
of their nervous system out of commission, also exhibited the usual emotional behaviour in anger, joy,
disgust and fear.

Such experimental evidence is amplified by observations reported on a patient who could feel no sensation
from the neck downward. The range of her experienced emotions was completely normal, despite the
lack of accompanying bodily sensations. A theory,
then, which claims that emotion is nothing more than
the experiencing of the particular bodily occurrences
which normally accompany it, finds no confirmation
experimentally when in the absence of these crucial
bodily changes and sensations ; there still results experienced emotion in human beings, and observable
emotional behaviour in animals.

Our other test question gives the same sort of answer.
It was found that when a certain substance, adrenalin,
known to be present in the body during fear, was
introduced artificially, it gave rise to the expected
bodily sensations, but the experienced ' flavour ' of
emotion was absent. The subject reported not that
he was afraid, but that he experienced sensations ' as
if he were afraid '. In other words, even though
palpitations, trembling, chilliness and oppression in

the chest were induced, these in themselves did not constitute the same experience as the genuine emotion.

The theory with which the modern physiologist has supplanted that of Lange and James, as a result of such experiments, considers changes in part of the brain, rather than the bodily changes *per se*, to be the crucial factor in emotion. Their positive evidence comes from patients whose emotional abnormalities accompany definite injury or diseased conditions in a particular area of the brain. As experimental psychologists, however, this is hardly our legitimate province, but the importance of such findings is that they again serve to remind us of the interconnection between all branches of investigations, the dependence of the psychological upon physiology, pathology and chemistry.

Returning, then, to our own field, we may give an example of experiments framed to help us understand the nature of emotions from another angle, experiments which are concerned with the essentially psychological characteristics, but which are in no way incompatible with the more recent physiological theory.

What will happen when a subject is continually thwarted in carrying out a task which he has undertaken ? In an experiment such as this the ' artificial ' aspect which we mentioned as a difficulty before, is reduced to a minimum ; and a very real anger results. The unwitting subject embarks on a task which he has every intention of finishing ; whenever he nears its completion, however, the experimenter manages to render it impossible. One such task may be the picking up of minute shavings and sawdust from a wooden floor, until not one remains. When, after very painstaking efforts, the floor is amazingly clean, the experimenter will deliberately upset the box and tell the subject his task is to pick them up again. Or the task may be to build a card house several stories high, but just as the last story goes on, the experimenter knocks against the table and down tumbles the pile, and such a performance will be repeated time and time again.

But, you will object, why does that make the subject angry ? Does he not know that it is only an experiment ? Yes, but he does not know it is an experiment on anger : what he does feel is that he is being hindered from doing his best, yet is held at his task by his promise to act as a subject. That is, he can neither complete his task and so be free, nor back out of the whole situation without being conspicuous and an admitted failure. Since he does not know that the tasks are made hopeless on purpose, his pride keeps him making ever new efforts. He is, in fact, kept in a state of tension which gradually becomes increasingly severe, with the result that an explosion of anger occurs. The subject may swear to himself or at the experimenter, knock down his own work, or stamp about the room. But when even such an explosion brings no real relief, when he is still held in precisely the same predicament, the expression of this anger may change. The subject may try to inhibit his outbursts in an attempt to remove or withdraw his most vulnerable 'self' from the unpleasant situation. If this is also unsuccessful, this attempt at isolation may be followed by a yet more drastic outburst, which in its turn, however, brings new tensions as a result of the shame felt for such excessively demonstrative behaviour.

"What an unpleasant experience," I can hear you say. For a few hours perhaps, but so illuminating in our attempt to understand emotional outbursts of anger that the subject undoubtedly forgives the experimenter when he is finally free and able to see the situation objectively.

Why is such an experiment important ? First, because of the genuine and spontaneous anger which it allows us to consider and record ; at the same time it is as nearly as possible a controlled and isolated situation. It is also important for our discussion because it shows that the concepts which we have been developing throughout these chapters are also applicable to that part of our mental life which we call 'ourselves', or in psychological terminology, our Egos ; that the self is amenable to the same kind of experimental treatment as we have seen applied to sight, sound, learning and memory.

If we retrace our steps for a moment, we may review some of the general ideas left behind in the first chapter. Broadly speaking, our contention there was that our only hope of giving an *explanation* of our experiences and of our ways of behaving, lay in being able to describe correctly the kinds of processes which must occur concomitantly in the brain and nervous system. One such explanation, which we did not subscribe to, was along purely mechanical lines, such that if we had accepted it we should have been forced to say that since bodily, nervous and brain processes were of the mechanical type, then our actions which resulted from them must be equally mechanical and automatic. In rejecting such an interpretation we were obliged to produce another in its place, and the interpretation which we submitted, while attaching equal importance to the concomitance of such processes during experience and behaviour, nonetheless gave to them a character altogether different from the purely mechanical one. The body was seen as a system, a whole, in which through the close interconnection of the myriad parts and sub-systems, interaction and mutual influence were the order of the day. The brain processes more especially were accredited with the freedom and spontaneity which is an essentially unmachine-like characteristic, for, having found processes in inorganic nature behaving in a way diametrically opposite to the ' penny-in-the-slot machine ', we postulated similar properties for these processes occurring in our brains. Our non-mechanical concepts helped us to understand many psychological phenomena in the previous chapters ; freed from a restricted mechanistic outlook it was not difficult to realize that nervous and brain processes underlay and accompanied all these mental and behavioural events, but it is perhaps more difficult to appreciate the fact that our knowledge of ourselves, those parts of experience which include the awareness of ' me ', *also* have some nervous counterpart, are also represented among the brain processes.

We return now to the experiments on anger, for it is here that they can help us, in that they show that these processes belonging to the ' self ' are processes similar to those which we have discussed before. Using our old terminology, we may say that they also seek to relieve tensions and to return to states of equilibrium, and continued tension will result, here as elsewhere, in an explosion. Moreover, as you would expect, these processes in the brain which belong to the Ego are not isolated ; they are closely connected with those processes which correspond to our knowledge of other individuals, events and things in the world around us. This means that the Ego processes cannot remain in equilibrium when the interconnection with these other processes is interfered with, when barriers are artificially introduced and pressure from within or without the system arises. In these experiments we see just this happening : here in a restricted total situation, where the subject is virtually hemmed in, where pressure is exerted by the experimenter and where the subject's adjustment to the situation is repeatedly destroyed, we find his Ego at odds with his surroundings and exploding with anger ; and may presumably postulate Ego-processes in the brain under tension seeking to relieve this tension as best they can.

Let us give one more concrete example concerning the relation of the Ego to the tasks which are undertaken in order to show more clearly what is meant by the statement that the Ego-processes are in close connection with others. Suppose I request my subject to perform the monotonous task of making small pencil strokes in groups of threes and fives on paper, and suppose that I give no indication of when this activity is to be ended. After an hour or so I shall find, as likely as not, that my subject will flatly refuse to continue on the ground that his hand is so over-tired that he can no longer hold the pencil. But, on a subsequent and similar experimental occasion I may find that the same subject will work for twice this length of time without any outburst of annoyance or exhibition of intense fatigue. Why ? Because on this second occasion it transpires that he has 'set himself a game' to see how long this monotonous task can be kept up. In other words the 'Ego' in this second case, instead of being engaged in something which evokes strain and tension, instead of being faced with a situation which is psychologically unending, is confronted with one which has a challenge and an objective to be striven for. But absolutely nothing has changed in the situation except the *relation* of that particular Ego to the task that it is doing, yet owing to this changed relationship, drudgery and increasing strain have altered to a constructive activity, that of establishing a record performance for this given task.

" I would like to ask a question," you may say at this point, " which has been bothering me for some time. Why do you always bring in the suggestion that the brain processes must be such and such ; why is it not enough to describe accurately what happens within a controlled experimental situation, and be content as a psychologist with psychological evidence ? " The answer is, of course, that we are making an attempt at explanation rather than being content with description, and as long as we remain solely in the realm of our actual experiences, we have no explanatory concepts. Granted that accurate description is necessary originally to tell us that this kind of connection between the self and the work the self does, exists, it cannot alone give us the kind of knowledge we are looking for. A child can tell you that when the button by the door is pushed the light will go on by the fire-place : an accurate description ; but the child cannot explain to you even what the necessary connections are. The average adult can describe the electric circuit, but will probably not have the vaguest idea of the concepts and mathematical symbols used to ' explain ' electricity as it is understood to-day. One of the aims of these chapters then has been to push the reader back beyond the stage of accepting psychological happenings in terms of press-the-button-and-the-light-goes-on, and to show him the necessity of searching for more adequate and fundamental causes for the experiences and actions which are his and his neighbour's, and which he takes so completely for granted.

For a full discussion on Emotion, C. Ruckmick's book, *Psychology of Feeling and Emotion* (New York, 1937), may be consulted.

Page 151 ff. A brilliant presentation of the James-Lange theory will be found in James' classical *Principles of Psychology* (New York and London).

The modern approach is presented by P. Bard in *The Handbook of General Experimental Psychology*, and also by Cannon in an article " The Lange-James Theory of Emotions ", *American Journal of Psychology*, Vol. 39, 1927, from which a few lines have been quoted.

,, 154 f. The experiments on anger performed by T. Dembo are described by K. Lewin in his *Dynamic Theory of Personality*.

,, 159 f. The experiments on monotonous work were performed by A. Karsten and are described by Lewin, *loc. cit.*

CHAPTER VIII

EXPERIMENTAL PSYCHOLOGY IN RETROSPECT

WE embarked on the writing of these chapters with a very definite aim in mind : namely, to free experimental psychology proper from the encroachments of its popular namesake and to provide some concrete examples of what the psychologist actually does. We attempted throughout to bear in mind the interested layman who asks in genuine perplexity whether it is really possible to make experiments with human beings. We have tried to show what constitutes a psychologist's problem, some of the methods by which he tackles it, and the significance of the more general conclusions which he reaches.

In an attempt to make such a discussion something more than the mere enumeration of specific cases, we have given them within a wider setting, advancing one possible approach to psychology as a background. Such a definite approach results in the selection of certain experiments rather than others, and has its drawbacks perhaps in presenting only comparatively few of the numerous experiments which could have been drawn upon to exemplify problems and methods.

163

Moreover, there is the danger that psychology will appear to the reader as a somewhat more unified subject than in fact it is, and to have developed smoothly and without interruption.

In this final chapter, therefore, we shall mention briefly some of the experimental landmarks or classics, regardless of whether or not they have withstood the test of time or subsequently proved to be as important as they seemed originally. As a matter of fact, in the development of any science or body of knowledge, the rise and fall of interest in certain topics, changes in methods and approach, are interesting in themselves. In psychology, as elsewhere, we find sometimes a veritable swing of the pendulum ; a new theory contradicts an older one, questions drop into the background and others supersede them, or a completely new outlook brings to life again the dead bones of an old problem. The general tenor of the age, the ' climate of opinion ' as it has been called, also plays its part in determining the course of development of an individual science. Certain investigations find support in what has been achieved in allied sciences, and thereby gain momentum, while others, being out of harmony, will be passed by without notice. Then again, there will be certain men who may be said to have changed the direction or the trend of thought, who have contributed ideas important enough to influence this general climate of opinion. As we make our rapid survey in this chapter it is of interest to keep such ideas in mind.

What then is our first landmark, or at what point can it be said that experimental psychology began ? The important date in the life of this young science seems to be that of its coming of age, of its reaching an independent status in the middle of the nineteenth century. It was not that this whole branch of thought remained unexplored until that time, but rather that it was so completely absorbed and overshadowed by its parents, philosophy and the physiology of the senses, that it made no claim for an independent existence.

On the philosophical side, general questions which we now consider of psychological interest had been discussed since the time of the Greeks : the relation of body to mind, the status of experience, the freedom of the will, what happens when we ' see ', the nature of memory and thought.   More particularly since the philosopher Locke in the seventeenth century, philosophic interest had centred around problems of the mind.

On the physiological side, particularly during the nineteenth century, there was a great deal discovered about the sense organs themselves, particularly the eye and the ear, and concerning what happened in these organs during the process of seeing and hearing. The men who are still associated with psychological theories of colour, Young, Helmholtz and Hering were not psychologists at all, but were interested in psychological problems from their own vantage-points of physics and physiology, and brought to bear upon these problems their own experimental procedures.

It is not often that one can say that at such and such a time a really new trend of thought came into existence, but when in 1860 Fechner, a philosopher and physicist, conceived the idea of treating a philosophical problem experimentally, he ushered in experimental psychology. The philosophic problem in this case was: How do we come to know the outside world, or how does the mental apprehend the physical? and the ' psycho-physical ' methods which Fechner evolved to handle this problem had all the hall-marks of scientific procedure.

In order to understand just what it was that Fechner contributed, we have to approach the problem in a rather general way. We all know that measurement in the physical world can be extremely accurate. Even if we make no pretence of being scientists, we can, for example, by making our units of measurement very small, arrive at an exact estimate of the weight of a piece of metal. We can also add to the original metal by a series of discrete steps, 0001 of an ounce let us say, making a *series* of weights all differing from each other by a constant, and in this case minute amount. But in addition to constructing this objective series of weights we can also place them on our hands so that we feel them, and we can say that this is heavier than that, and so on, so that we also get a scale or series of discrete and different *experiences*. But whereas the series in the physical world is measur-

able and objective, my scale, or your scale is still in
the mind's eye, subjective and unscientific.

Nonetheless the question arises, Does this scale of
experience correspond unit for unit, or in any other
way, with the units in the physical world? Because,
if it does, or if any constant relationship can be shown
to hold between units or ' bits ' of experience and such
recognized units as grams, ounces, decibels, ergs and
so on, then, if they can be equated reliably, there
should be some unit of measurement in psychology
after all. And since it had always been assumed
that psychology could never be a science for the sole
reason that mental life could never have a unit whereby
mental life could be accurately measured, anyone who
provided psychology with such a unit would have given
it an important tool for developing quantitatively.

But you will ask, does such a unit for unit corre-
spondence actually exist between these units in the
physical and mental worlds? The answer is No: for
all of our senses, not only that of touch, there are
physical increments which are far too small to have
any effect or produce any corresponding change in
experience; moreover, one and the same addition
physically may be experienced as a change on one
occasion and not on another, depending on other
factors in the whole situation. However, and this is
the point to which we have been coming for a long
time, *some* constant relationship exists between these
two series, which may be expressed in this way:
the subjective steps, or the differences in experience,

depend on the relation of the added (or subtracted) physical unit to the original amount.

This may look formidable, but a simple example will make it clear : If I put on your hand a weight of 200 grams, and then substitute for it one of 202 grams, there will be no change in your experience, 202 grams will not feel heavier to you than, or different from, the first weight ; in other words, your ' experienced scale ' has not changed in accordance with the change in the physical world. But if I put on your hand a weight of 4 grams, and then changed that to a weight of 6 grams, again as you see adding 2 grams in the second weight, this time you will experience a change, finding the second weight different and heavier than the first. Why ? Because the relation of 2 grams to 200 grams and to 4 grams is entirely different. 2 grams is only a one-hundredth part of 200 grams, but it is half of 4 grams.

We can express this slightly differently, as Fechner did, by saying that in order for the experienced changes to increase or decrease, step by step, unit by unit, or in arithmetical progression, the physical object must be increased or decreased by a constant fraction of itself, that is in geometrical progression. This constant fraction, it so happens, is different for each of the senses.

Not all of the facts mentioned above were discovered by Fechner, but it was he who formulated the relationship and gave it its more general significance by pointing out what it implied. Moreover, and perhaps most important for psychology at that time, he devised the methods which measured these ' steps ' of experience. We shall not attempt to discuss these beyond saying that experiment, coupled with mathematical treatment, was necessary in order to equate these ' just noticeable differences ', as they were called, with the specific physical unit. And so it became an accepted psychological dictum that there was a unit of mental life, known as the ' sensation ', and that an unbroken series of these sensations would be established by way of the ' just noticeable differences ' which in turn could be equated with known physical changes.

It may seem ironical, after we have developed this thought at some length, to say that, in the light of our present knowledge, very little significance is attached to this ' unit ' of mental life. Furthermore, that it has not proved for psychology the expected open sesame into the realms of the quantitative sciences. At that time, however, the importance of such an approach cannot be overrated : psychology, emancipated, started on a career of measurement ; and, as you will remember, one of the purposes of this chapter was to discuss these psychological landmarks regardless of whether or not they still dominated the psychological horizon.

Fechner, we said, had inaugurated an era of measurement : another province in which a quantitative approach became the order of the day was that of the Reaction Time. It became all important to

psychologists for a time to know, with a great degree
of accuracy, ' how long ' it took for the various mental
functions to occur. The problem was brought to
their notice in an interesting way : astronomers in
their work had discovered that the time taken between
seeing a star at a certain point and recording it, differed
for different individuals. The psychologist therefore
began a series of measurements, in 1/1000 of a second,
in all the sensory and motor phases of behaviour,
with emphasis also on the comparison of different
individual performances.

A simple experiment would be something of this
sort : the subject would be asked to press a button
' immediately ' he saw a light flash, or heard the sound
of a bell. Just what ' immediately ' was for this
particular subject in this particular sensory field
would then be recorded. This would be achieved by
having the stimulus, let us say, the electric bell, and
the button all on the same electric circuit, which
would also include a clock which registers in 1/1000
of a second. This apparatus being so constructed
that when the bell sounds it sets the hands of the
clock whirling round, and when the subject presses
the button they stop, showing the interval which
has elapsed or the time taken by the subject to respond
to the sound. After the various simple modes of
behaviour had been examined in this way, after
norms had been arrived at, and individual differences
investigated, this same apparatus and technique were
used to examine more complex mental functions ; for

example, how long does a process of choice or discrimination take? The subject in this case would have to press one button on being shown a red light, let us say, and another on being shown a green, the time difference between this and the simple response to red alone, would give the amount of time needed to discriminate between red and green.

Reaction times, like the psycho-physical methods, had their day, but a purely quantitative approach could not remain in the forefront of psychological thought indefinitely, for it led to a circumscribed province rather than the opening up of wide vistas.

Fechner's influence however, in addition to setting the fashion for meticulous measurement, was being felt elsewhere, for he had also, you will remember, drawn attention to that newly discovered psychological unit, the sensation. So we find these elementary experiences, these bricks out of which all mental life was presumably built, these psychological atoms, being subjected to a thorough scrutiny. Since this sensation was the unit of experience it followed that it must contain only one quality, therefore the ordinary experiences of daily life were broken up in an attempt to isolate the various sensations which were supposed to be amalgamated to compose them. For example, how is pure ' redness ' experienced, redness when isolated from the meaning, shape, brightness and texture of the red thing ? Or again, what is the pure sensation of brightness, or pain, or feeling happy for that matter, when all the other elements are shaken free from them ?

Expert subjects examined their consciousness in order to describe these ' pure ' sensations : wetness, for example, they analysed down to the sensation of cold, plus the sensation of pressure. Pleasure, when broken up in this way, was described as bright pressures. The psychologist's tool or method during these experiments was his own ' introspection ', the turning of his attention on to his own everyday experiences and analysing them in a cold-blooded fashion. The more highly trained the subject the better for the experimenter, and a highly trained subject was one who could reduce everyday experiences most thoroughly to the elements which they were presumably made up of.

Let us go back for a moment to those general tendencies which were mentioned earlier in this chapter. This emphasis on measurement, and this preoccupation with detailed analysis of the psychological unit, are in marked contrast to the previous inclusion of psychological problems within philosophical speculation. They illustrate a sharp break in the continuity of the thought which can be called psychological. That the general ' climate of opinion ' in the late nineteenth century fostered ingenious methods of measurement is also certain ; and it may also be said that Fechner influenced the thought of the time and of subsequent thinking very considerably by bringing within the same system two apparently mutually exclusive realms, the physical and the mental.

The subsequent swing of the pendulum away from an exclusive preoccupation with sensations marks another break in the development of psychological thought. As we mentioned in another chapter, such a purely ' one-man affair ' as the reports of these highly trained subjects could not be considered scientific. Consequently a wave of protest, voiced very loudly by the Behaviourists, whom we have also mentioned, swept over the field of psychology. At one stage, in their anxiety to purge psychology of all that prevented it from being objective, these extremists actually went so far as to deny the existence of consciousness itself.

But there were other reactions, other changing foci of interest even before the somewhat extreme one of Behaviourism. One came in the insistence that the individual was a living, acting organism, and that his total activity, rather than the fabric of his consciousness as evidenced in the preoccupation with sensation, should be the central theme of psychology : such an approach was known as that of the Functional Psychologists.

Then there was the protest, voiced by some psychologists, and amplified by the stentorian voice of Freud and his followers, against the purely rational aspect of mankind which was being studied with complete disregard for the fundamental biological urges.

In Germany, the movement known as Gestalt theory, the fundamental concepts of which have undoubtedly coloured the presentation of experiments in these chapters, raised their voices against the artificial aspect of the sensation, against the kind of analysis which produced such an unreal element, and at the same time against a mechanistic outlook which denuded human life of its essential meaningfulness, and which was based on an unnecessarily restricted model of the physical universe.

Experimental psychology, as a whole, is more concerned with the nature of mind and behaviour in general, than with the differences between individual minds and modes of action : nonetheless, mention must be made of a wave of interest which centred in investigations on individual differences in intelligence, as measured by intelligence tests. These intelligence tests have become a branch of psychology in their own right, distinct from the experimental province; they have, however, their own more strictly experimental side, and their general theoretical aspects. One such theoretical question is whether intelligence is some one general ability, or factor, permeating all, or nearly all of the activities of the individual ; or whether it is really the net result of various separate capacities. Strange as it may seem the battleground of this controversy, on its theoretical side, is in the field of mathematical statistics. The tests themselves are designed for either general intelligence or for certain specific abilities such as music, mechanics, arithmetic, language and so forth ; and tests exist for infants, children of all ages, college students and adults.

In the first chapter we found it necessary to clear the ground by stating ' what psychology was *not* ' :

now that we have shown the psychologist at work, and now that you are somewhat more familiar with the field, it is fitting that we attempt the more difficult task of suggesting ' what experimental psychology *is* '.

The province of psychology, I think you will agree, includes a study of the actions and experiences of human beings, and the behaviour of infants and animals from whose experience we cannot draw additional information. But we have seen that because this province is a common one to the inorganic, the organic and the mental, because as we have previously paraphrased, it is the juncture where physical nature, life and mind meet, it frequently happens that the psychologist must go beyond his own subject-matter in order to understand it.

The need for this we have mentioned in almost every chapter ; we may formulate it once more in this way : we cannot go very far back in our series of cause and effect if we stay at the level of experience or observed behaviour alone. I step aside *because* I see a car coming, cause and effect ; but how did I ' see ' the car ? Light rays initiated certain processes : and what kind of processes ? Already we are outside the realm of psychology proper. Or again, I feel angry *because* you upset the ink on my manuscript : but how did the seeing of the upset ink cause the emotion of anger with its bodily manifestations ? Pure psychology cannot answer this question without more facts, and we have to turn to the physiologist.

And there is another realm into which, whether he likes it or not, the psychologist makes excursions, namely into that of the philosopher. Even those psychologists who most vigorously decry this, are none-theless constructing a consistent philosophical setting in the mechanical background which they give to their psychological facts.

The psychologist then studies behaviour and experi-ences within a wider setting. But *how* does he study them ? It is at this point that we must justify the use of the word 'experimental'. When the psycho-logist makes an experiment he asks a question : the best and most pertinent questions will, as a rule, be those framed after consideration of what theoretical points need verifying or amplifying. Similarly an answer to an experimental problem, even if this pro-blem has been a restricted one, will be valuable to the extent that it can be incorporated within a wider setting and to the extent that it can lead to the formulation of new and relevant questions.

This does not mean that the psychologist must experiment solely in order to establish his theoretical approach at all costs. Rather this theoretical approach must live and grow in accordance with the results of his experimental findings, that is in accordance with ' stubborn facts.' In order that these facts may be reliable, an experiment must be controlled, but the psychologist must be aware that his experimental sub-ject-matter is far more difficult to control than is that of the sciences on which he models his work.

He must not expect, therefore, to find that all the problems which he ought and needs to tackle can be squeezed into the strictest scientific mould. On the other hand, where most accurate control can be made, as for example in experiments in perception, where the factors which cannot be controlled are irrelevant to the issue in hand, at such places progress most similar to that of the natural sciences can be made, and what is gained there may be utilized at other levels. In common with all experimentalists, of course, the psychologist must be open-minded, ready to be led to conclusions other than those which he may have anticipated.

Experimental psychology, then, may not lend itself to easy and spectacular presentation, nor is it a patent medicine for all mental ills, but it does have a part to play in the drama of our progressive understanding of ourselves and the world we live in.

The reader interested in the history of psychology is
advised to turn to the following books: J. C. Flugel, *A
Hundred Years of Psychology* (London, 1934); and E. G.
Boring, *History of Experimental Psychology* (New York,
1930).

INDEX